From a portrait by Lilla Cabot Perry

EDWIN ARLINGTON ROBINSON

By
BEN RAY REDMAN

ROBERT M. McBRIDE & COMPANY
NEW YORK ::   ::   ::   ::   ::   1928

PS
3535
O25
Z8
R̄obinson
R

11215

EDWIN ARLINGTON ROBINSON
—
PRINTED IN THE UNITED STATES OF AMERICA

For

F. I. R.

The makers of epigrams, of phrases, of pages—of all more or less brief judgments—assuredly waste their time when they sum up any one of all mankind; and how do they squander it when their matter is a poet! They may hardly describe him; nor shall any student's care, or psychologist's formula, or man-of-letters' summary, or wit's sentence define him. Definitions, because they must not be inexact or incomprehensive, sweep too wide; and out of the mere describer's range and capture he may escape by as many doors as there are outlets from a forest.

ALICE MEYNELL.

EDWIN ARLINGTON ROBINSON

I

WERE the business at hand to point a moral rather than to adorn a tale, our subject would be perfect for the purpose. The years of Mr. Robinson's conscientious labor have been long enough, his success has been sufficiently belated, and his final triumph has been notable enough to furnish forth a splendid sermon that would rest upon the honored text of a copy-book axiom. No whim of public taste decreed his elevation, no planned audacity won him sudden shocked attention; at no Byronic dawn did fame salute the opening of his eyelids. His has been the long, hard road; the copy-book road, so innocent of short-cuts. His only peer among American poets, if peer he has, was a cherished scandal before he was a cherished author; the barbaric yawp that raised him from obscurity is a byword to readers who have never opened "Leaves of Grass." But if the name of Edwin Arlington Robinson has ever been linked with scandal, the fact has been blotted from our records; and the voice that has raised *him* from obscurity is one of such moderation, such careful modulation, that only attentive ears were first aware of it; and the circle of those early readers has been widened at a pace so leisurely as to arouse at once delight and despair in the breast of the ardent Robinsonian, who would, like all idolators, make his idol known to the whole world, while yet desiring to reserve him for most private worship.

But that is history, now. The oracles have spoken with quite unoracular unanimity and no Delphic ambiguity at all. The years of honest toil have yielded their reward, in sales that a popular novelist would deem invisible, in prizes pleasingly tangible, in honorary degrees, and in behests to lecture before divers centers of palpitating female culture. Besides, the poet may now enjoy the dubious delight of reading long reviews and little books devoted to his life and works. At least once a year he may seriously confront his own serious countenance in two-score literary supplements; and thumbing the index of any recent anthology of contemporary poetry, he may experience the same minor satisfaction that the average man can procure only by thumbing a copy of the telephone book. His name is sure to be there, writ large indeed, for all that it is set in the same type as its fellows. For the miracle has come to pass: Edwin Arlington Robinson is admittedly our greatest living poet, and some would call him the greatest poet that this country has produced. Worth what it is, the title is his own, though the donors may find it one more difficult to define than to bestow.

And it is a miracle of a sort, for Robinson has won to his present position during one of the most turbulent periods in poetry, in all art, that this country or any other country has ever known. Surrounded by mutinous banners, amidst a din of strange cacophonous music, he has moved quietly to a height unscaled by any of the mutineers. While funeral orations have been read above the poor dead forms of traditional poetry, he has persisted in believing them to be alive and well adapted to his uses. His acclamation by his contemporaries is as odd as if some stern, unbending seigneur of the old régime had been hoisted triumphantly to the shoulders of red-capped citizens before the Bastille in the year 1789.

That he is constantly associated, in the minds of critics and of readers, with the rebels of 1913, is a mistake for which chronology must answer. Our poetic "renaissance" was in full swing when "The Man Against the Sky" brought its author his first wide recognition in 1916, but with that renaissance he had, precisely, no connection. From the sudden torrent of poetic energy that burst upon a defenceless republic in the second decade of the twentieth century, Robinson derived no strength or inspiration. He was a lonely pioneer, the true voortrekker of another poet. The man who published "Flammonde" and "John Gorham" and "Bewick Finzer," in 1916, had written "John Evereldown" and "Luke Havergal" and "Richard Cory" between the years 1890 and 1896. Tilbury Town had found its singer twenty years before "Des Imagistes" found its public. When the passion for experimentation in poetry became epidemic, Robinson had long since learned what experiments could teach him. Before the poetic babes of 1913 had learned to prattle, he had come to man's estate. And so it may be asserted with all confidence that Edwin Arlington Robinson's writings would have differed no jot from what they are, had the recent renaissance of our poetry never been. That he may have profited, in readers, from the generally awakened interest in all forms of poetic utterance is probably true, and that his influence has been considerable is unquestionable, but all that is quite beside the present point.

Neither in spirit, nor intention, nor production, has he ever belonged to any definable movement; for his is not the temperament that blossoms in the forcing atmosphere of cliques and coteries. With those who name him the prolocutor of New England, I would argue; but in his aloof self-respect, his dignified independence, he is a veritable Yankee. To the organized voices of the future he has been as serenely indifferent as he was in his youth to the organized voices of the immediate past, speaking through the mouths of Emerson, Longfellow, Lowell and Bryant; as indifferent as he was to contemporary voices across the sea. And this was his strength, for American poetry, during the priesthood of the Boston Brahmins, suffered from the same malady that sterilized French poetry during the two centuries following Racine: the formula was imitation, not of the Aristotelian, but of a lower kind; and the succeeding generation of American poets scarcely improved matters by transferring their imitation to models who were themselves imitators. When Miss Lowell said of the group that made Boston what it is not to-day, "They were English poets, in the sense that

America was still a literary province of the Mother Country," she limited the application of her remark rather more strictly than was needful.

Provincial Edwin Arlington Robinson never was: he aped the romantic ardor no more than he affected the romantic collar; when he looked at nature it was not through Wordsworth's eyes; and the waters upon the strand of Dover Beach told him nothing of "the turbid ebb and flow of human misery" that he had not already learned from the rising and receding tides of Maine. The sources from which he drank deepest were so old as to be the property of all men, and the private property of none. Naturally and without self-consciousness he accepted the heritage of a great tradition, that bid a poet stand squarely on his own feet and view the world of men with the candid vision of a Hesiod or a Chaucer. Echoes there are, to be sure, in his poetry; but what there is of imitation in that first public volume, "Children of the Night," is the very minimum of second-hand matter that must be handled by even the greatest in their youth. "Her Eyes" is nearly as bad as it could be, judged by the standards that Robinson has since established for himself; indeed, it might well have been written, some years later, by Robert W. Service in a slightly more inspired moment than that which produced "New Year's Eve." And "Ballad by the Fire" might well have been penned gracefully by Austin Dobson. But the poet had already found himself when he set down the strange haunting music of "John Evereldown," the nobly simple stanzas of "Luke Havergal," the cryptic anecdote of "Cliff Klingenhagen," and the terse tribute of "George Crabbe." Recall the last two verses of the first:

"But why are you going so late, so late,—
  Why are you going, John Evereldown?
  Though the road be smooth and the way be straight,
  There are two long leagues to Tilbury Town,
  Come in by the fire, old man, and wait.
  Why do you chatter out there by the gate?
  And why are you going so late, so late,—
  Why are you going, John Evereldown?"

"I follow the women wherever they call,—
  That's why I'm going to Tilbury Town.
  God knows if I pray to be done with it all,
  But God is no friend to John Evereldown.
  So the clouds may come and the rain may fall,
  The shadows may creep and the dead men crawl,—
  But I follow the women wherever they call,
  And that's why I'm going to Tilbury Town."

And the end of "Luke Havergal":

There is the western gate, Luke Havergal,
There are the crimson leaves upon the wall.
Go, for the winds are tearing them away,—
Nor think to riddle the dead words they say,
Nor any more to feel them as they fall;
But go, and if you trust her she will call.
There is the western gate, Luke Havergal.

These are fragments, but let the anecdote and the tribute be quoted in entirety:

Cliff Klingenhagen had me in to dine
With him one day; and after soup and meat,
And all the other things there were to eat,
Cliff took two glasses and filled one with wine
And one with wormwood. Then, without a sign
For me to choose at all, he took the draught
Of bitterness himself, and lightly quaffed
It off, and said the other one was mine.

And when I asked him what the deuce he meant
By doing that, he only looked at me
And smiled, and said it was a way of his.
And though I know the fellow, I have spent
Long time a-wondering when I shall be
As happy as Cliff Klingenhagen is.

And now George "Crabbe":

Give him the darkest inch your shelf allows,
Hide him in lonely garrets, if you will,—
In spite of all fine science disavows,
But his hard, human pulse is throbbing still
With the sure strength that fearless truth endows.
Of his plain excellence and stubborn skill
There yet remains what fashion cannot kill,
Though years have thinned the laurel from his brows.

Whether or not we read him, we can feel
From time to time the vigor of his name
Against us like a finger for the shame
And emptiness of what our souls reveal
In books that are as altars where we kneel
To consecrate the flicker, not the flame.

These specific quotations thrust abruptly into the
midst of general prefatory remarks will not prove in-

apposite if they drive home the fact that Edwin Arlington Robinson was as ripe for critical discovery in 1896 as he was in 1916. In "Children of the Night" there was no single work of the sustained beauty and strength that, twenty years later, were to characterize "The Man Against the Sky" or "Ben Jonson Entertains a Man from Stratford"—and certainly there was nothing which foreshadowed the serene accomplishment of "Merlin"—but there were half a dozen poems that, in their kinds, Robinson has scarcely bettered since, and there were a dozen that pointed like true arrows along the road his talents were to take. The whole collection, with a few negligible exceptions, bore witness to the objectivity that has always characterized Robinson's attitude towards his poetical subjects. Here, said the little book as plainly as sound words could say it, is a poet not so much interested in his own emotions and character as in the characters and emotions of other men. Here is a poet who is not content to interpret and explain life subjectively through the experiences, actual and mental, of a single individual, but one who is impelled to scrutinize the human being in as many guises and situations as he can find him, and then translate the results of observation, understanding and analysis into poetry. From the immediate life around him, Robinson peopled his first book with the "imaginary" characters of John Evereldown, Luke Havergal, Aaron Stark, Cliff Klingenhagen, Charles Carville, Fleming Helphenstine, Richard Cory, and Reuben Bright; and he created a place for their lives to be played out; Tilbury Town, which was founded eighteen years before ground was broken along Spoon River. From the pages of literature he summoned Zola, Verlaine, Thomas Hood and George Crabbe, thereby forming the nucleus of an historical company which later, as book followed book, was to include Ben Jonson, Erasmus, Lincoln, Lazarus, Saint Paul and Rembrandt.

His preoccupation with humanity was strikingly apparent, and his predilection for certain companionable types was equally so. It was not to the apparently flawless that he turned most readily, but to the flawed; not to the greatly blessed, but to the somewhat cursed. The first inhabitants of Tilbury Town included a "skirt-crazed reprobate," a lover whose only hope lay in western skies, a miser whose eyes were "little dollars in the dark," who never laughed save when a word of pity for him drifted to his ears; a man of wealth who put a bullet through his head; a sorry wreck whose "mouth redeemed his insufficient eyes" that never spoke their message till he died; a butcher who "Tore down to the slaughter house" that he might kill the pain his wife's death caused him. And what of the historical characters? Zola,—hated and reviled because he put "The compromising chart of hell" before our eyes. Hood,— "The man who cloaked his bitterness within this winding-sheet of puns and pleasantries." George Crabbe,— despite whose "hard, human pulse" the "years have thinned the laurel from his brows. . . ." Verlaine,—

Why do you dig like long-clawed scavengers
To touch the covered corpse of him that fled
The uplands for the fens, and rioted
Like a sick satyr with doom's worshippers?

Come! let the grass grow there; and leave his verse
To tell the story of the life he led.
Let the man go: let the dead flesh be dead,
And let the worms be its biographers.

Yes, his chief preoccupations and predilections were
apparent from the first. And so, too, was his basic attitude toward all existence, his philosophy, if we must
call it that. We find it in the title poem of that early
volume.

> For those that never know the light,
> The darkness is a sullen thing;
> And they, the Children of the Night,
> Seem lost in Fortune's winnowing.

But we cannot admit there is no light, even though
it is obscured; for were we to do that,

> 'Twere better, ere the sun go down
> Upon the first day we embark,
> In life's imbittered sea to drown,
> Than sail forever in the dark.

And in "Credo," "Two Sonnets" and the "Octaves,"
the same theme is played upon with minor variations.
At times the note of hope, at times the tones of despair
are dominant; frequently they contend within the single
poem. Here is the second of the "Octaves":

> Tumultuously void of a clean scheme
> Whereon to build, whereof to formulate,
> The legion life that riots in mankind
> Goes ever plunging upward, up and down,

Most like some crazy regiment at arms,
Undisciplined of aught but Ignorance,
And ever led resourcelessly along
To brainless carnage by drunk trumpeters.

And here is the last:

Here by the windy docks I stand alone,
But yet companioned. There the vessel goes,
And there my friend goes with it; but the wake
That melts and ebbs between that friend and me
Love's earnest is of Life's all-purposeful
And all-triumphant sailing, when the ships
Loose their fretful chains and swing
Forever from the crumbled wharves of Time.

The conflict in the poet's mind is crystal clear, and its mechanism quite familiar. The clash arises from the measureless discrepancy between life experienced and life desired; the forces involved are chilling reason and warming faith, each impotent to conquer wholly, each incapable of complete surrender. This interplay, everywhere present in Robinson's work, demands serious consideration, which must be postponed for the moment. The fact to be emphasized at present is that the poet's first book revealed the matter, manner, and philosophy that were to serve him in maturity. Here was a new voice speaking through old forms. Here was a poet who turned the ancient ballad to the purposes of psychological realism, who made the villanelle bear a weight that none before him had entrusted to its slender form, who fashioned sonnets as vigorously as though a thousand sonneteers had not preceded him.

Yet, really, when we say the forms in which he expressed himself were old, we perpetuate a critical fallacy; for the fact is that every poem, every work of art, is a new "form." Divested of style and substance, matter and manner, "Form" remains no more than the expression of a classification or a measurement. To speak of two sonnets as identical forms is convenient but inaccurate, for there is no such thing as the sonnet in itself; there are only individual sonnets, and the change of even a single word in any one produces a different whole.

It is only when we have recognized this basic fact that we may make use of the critical apparatus of classification, history and comparison. Yet we must employ such apparatus to a certain extent, even though it be a compromise with truth, or else rest inarticulate. To view any work of art in complete isolation is an unattainable ideal to a man who has ever viewed another work of art before; to explain any work of art entirely in terms of itself is equally impossible. So, if we speak about such matters at all, we must fall back upon the old machinery of classification, historical correlation, and translation of the unfamiliar into familiar terms. Admitting, once for all, that a work of art is its own, and only perfect, interpretation and explanation, the critic is yet constrained by the very nature of his task to essay the impossibility of explaining a work of art from without. His, necessarily, is the exterior and imperfect view; perfection in this case lies with the artist, who has done his explaining from within.

But here we become involved in a kind of critical

metaphysics that provokes endless and perhaps un-profitable discussion. Our concern, for the time being, is to fix upon the questions that a modest critic may presume to pose and answer. That these questions should be as simple and direct as possible seems desir-able. Artistic chaos results inevitably in critical chaos, and such is assuredly the state in which we live to-day. But if there is any lesson we should have learned of late, it is that there are certain things which criticism can not yet claim to do. Until, for example, the æsthetic sensation is isolated, in fulfillment of T. S. Eliot's opti-mism, the appreciation of poetry, as of all art, will re-main highly personal and to a certain degree incom-municable. To explain why

> Thou still unravished bride of quietness,
> Thou foster child of silence and slow time.

are beautiful lines, is to catch the rainbow and wear it for a scarf. Seized upon, the lines are resolved not into mist like the rainbow but into small hard words that yield no loveliness. As the worthy Dr. Johnson remarked in a quite different connection: "Pound St. Paul's church into atoms, and consider any single atom; it is, to be sure, good for nothing; but put all these atoms together, and you have St. Paul's church."

Well, the pounding method has long since gone out of date, but there was something to be said for it. Those murderers of poetry, skilled in the arts of a Quintilian or a Puttenham, did indeed slay their lines by the thousands; but they experienced a glow of complacent assurance that their harassed successors can never know. However wrong they may have been, they knew that they were right. The critic of to-day, we are assured, must simply feel, and then describe as best he may what he has felt. No more than that is fashionable; Anatole France and Lemaitre have not fought in vain; the world is safe for the posterity of Sainte-Beuve. Perhaps. But this method of avoiding our grandfathers' errors seems somehow to smack of cowardice, for they at least had the courage to fix their eyes firmly upon the object to be criticized, while we elude the issue by retiring behind expressions of personal prejudice and opinion that no man can reasonably contradict. So long as we think or feel that a thing is so, then for us it is so; and that is the ultimate argument of subjective criticism. It will be refuted, perhaps, only when science eventually undermines the subjective base of our current metaphysics.

Meanwhile we have pulled lustily at the ancient props, and the world is momentarily about our ears. Our only refuge is simplicity and humility. Our subject, and our object, is a poet. Very well. Of what themes does he write? What is his attitude toward them? Has he written much or little, and is his work even or uneven so far as we may judge it by its own standards? Is growth or decline perceptible in his career? And where does he appear to stand amid his contemporaries, or in the greater company to which he belongs with all his predecessors? These questions we may safely ask, I think. How well they may be answered is another matter.

We have already skirted the nature of Robinson's first work. A few biographical facts must now be recorded; and are necessarily few, for the story of this poet's life is almost entirely the story of his writing. It is, however, of prime importance that we should have some clear idea of the literary world in which the youthful poet found himself. What men were dwelling on the heights in those days, and who were the mighty ones of the market-place?

II

THE sixties rather than the seventies of the nineteenth century claimed Edwin Arlington Robinson as their child by the margin of a few days only, for he was born on the 22nd of December, 1869. His birthplace was the small Maine village of Head Tide, more picturesque than notable; his father was a dealer in grain. And apparently the elder Robinson was a merchant of esteemed abilities, for the offer of a directorship in the Gardiner bank caused him to move himself and his family to the larger community when the future poet was scarcely a year old.

One who has had no personal acquaintance with Maine towns and villages during the closing decades of the last century may only speculate as to the possible influences of this early environment. Clement Wood has assured us that both Head Tide and Gardiner "at that time were bleak with an air of seventeenth-century Puritanism," and Amy Lowell, who seems to have had some personal knowledge of the latter place in more recent days, has written: "I know of no place in America so English in atmosphere as Gardiner. Standing on the broad, blue Kennebec, the little town nestles proudly beside that strange anomaly in an American city—the Manor House." Miss Lowell has employed the Great House, standing bravely in decay beside the growing town, as a symbol of the world into which the poet was born, and she has hinted at what young Robinson may have thought of it, and of the contrast in which it played a part. We have no more than speculation to guide us here, but we may assume at least that the Gardiner mansion was for the boy a visible and tangible embodiment of romance,—romance of a sort not easily discoverable at that time in Maine or in any other of the United States. Contemplating the Manor House, the future poet contemplated the past itself, and turning his eyes to the busy town he may have become conscious for the first time of an eternal drama and an eternal tragedy. Whether or not the house of Gardiner may be accurately identified with "The House on the Hill," the fact is that this early poem may well express Robinson's realization of, and his resignation to, the kind of tragedy of which the Great House was a symbol. And at the same time this poem demonstrates, as others have observed, the strange new use to which the poet could turn so blithe a form as the villanelle. The last verse tells the story:

> There is ruin and decay
> In the House on the Hill:
> They are all gone away,
> There is nothing more to say.

But this, you may remark, is no just description of the Gardiner House as it was in the days of Robinson's youth; the fortunes of the owner had declined, but his ancestral hall was not abandoned. True, but we may accept it as an example of how a poet deals with and transmutes his material, how he reacts to suggestions

from the world around him. Those who knew the
Manor House might not recognize its depiction in "The
House on the Hill," but no more would the inhabitants
of Gardiner recognize their own community in the poet's
"Tilbury Town." Yet there is little doubt that the
one is an image, a poet's image, of the other. Flammonde, Bewick Finzer and Luke Havergal did not walk
the Gardiner streets, but there did walk there the
prototypes of these imaginary folk. They were present in the germ, in the suggestion; there were men of
Gardiner who, as captured by the poet's mind, might
well have been Flammonde, Finzer and Havergal.

It is, indeed, this act of transmutation which must
contribute essentially to all poetry; for realism in
poetry is a contradiction in terms. As John Livingston
Lowes, more broadly generalizing, has phrased it: "For
art deals in *illusion*. Literal accuracy, even when possible, is art's undoing. A tree painted with all sedulous
exactness as a tree, would never give the tree at all;
painted as Corot paints it, or as Rembrandt etches it,
it's more a tree than if it were a tree." Of late we have
seen stark realism essayed, and we have noted the result:
most quick oblivion for experiments and experimenters
alike. At present it is a fashion to transmute reality
not into the beautiful but into the bizarre, yet there is
still a hint of the divine alchemy in the process; and so
long as the crucible is put to use at all, all is not lost.
But when we let base metal pass current as minted gold,
then poetry and all art will be dead.

Robinson possesses this vital gift of transmutation
in a high degree, whether he is dealing with the historical

figure of a Flemish painter, with the legendary characters of the Arthurian cycle, or with the protagonists of a modern triangle-drama. He is an acute depictor of human types, a shrewd doctor of souls, a sharp psychologist,—granted; but he can conduct his operations only in an atmosphere which throws a cloak of romance, or illusion, over the whole proceeding. He conveys his characters, whoever they may be, whatever their time, into a region of his own creation; he sets them down within the confines of his own subjective universe. The dramas of "Merlin" and of "Roman Bartholow" are played out in a world fraught with infinite suggestions and a myriad romantic implications. His garrulous Captain Craig talks on until he assumes epic proportions; the figure of Avon is that of a man walking in a dream; his Rembrandt is as darkly eloquent of mystery as the painter's oils. In short, Robinson is a poet. Temperament is his, and the command of verbal magic. Through the one he views the world, and by the other he gives form and substance to his vision.

So Robinson grew up in Gardiner, Maine, viewing that staid New England community from the clarifying distance that his temperament made possible, attended the local high school, and in due course moved on to the halls of Harvard University. What he may have learned there, between 1891 and 1893, is a matter for conjecture; but we may assume that the reward of his attendance was the bare modicum which an educational institution framed for average mediocrity usually offers to exceptional youth. If his masters pointed out ways whereby he might satisfy his obvious passion for biography, for knowledge of his fellow men, they did their part. In any event, he had scant need of them.

His college career ended in 1893, when circumstance compelled him to relinquish the joys of formal education for the business of earning a livelihood; and the years 1897 and 1898 found him in New York City, engaged in that oldest of struggles, for which nature seems to equip few poets generously. Meantime he had issued his small paper-covered, privately-printed book of forty-odd pages, with the notice, "This book is dedicated to any man, woman, or critic who will cut the edges of it. I have done the top"; and, in the following year, "The Children of the Night," running to more than a hundred pages of text, and more pretentiously encased in muslin-covered boards that were bright with decorations of red and green. He had openly declared himself a practitioner of the least lucrative of all professions, and he was to remain true to his vows. He might play at inspecting growing subways, or, when memory prodded him, draw a pay-check from the New York Custom House; but the really serious business of all his days was to be the writing of poetry. What, then, were the general features of that poetic, literary world into which he made his modest entrance? What were the critics and readers of his day demanding; what brows wore the laurel crown?

The state of American poetry during the closing years of the last century was neither satisfactory, exciting nor promising; only the shrewdest of observers could have noted in the faint ruffling of placid waters the prelude of wide storms. With the last page of his American Anthology in type, Edmund Clarence Stedman, himself not memorable for virile utterance, declared that what his country needed was "adult, male verse," and he found little consolation in contemporary promise. In one of the most recent summaries of those barren years, Carl and Mark Van Doren have stated the case succinctly:

"By the year 1890 the most famous American poets had joined, in varying degrees, the ranks of the classics. To say nothing of Poe, who died young, Bryant, Lanier, Longfellow, and Emerson were already dead; and Lowell, Whitman, Whittier, and Holmes, were at the end of their careers. There were, indeed, numerous writers of verse who had some reputation, but the public was right in feeling that these were minor poets, earnest or dainty survivors from more energetic days. No one of them had been shaped by the great national struggles of the past century and no one of them gave voice to the newer national ideals which were demanding expression. For the most part, they were content to sing pretty songs about remote emotions or to argue in meter about established ideas. They might, of course, have been significant, without being strikingly national; but in this respect also they fell below the level of great poetry. Too many of them seemed to feel that it was their duty to limit their utterance to subjects which were polite or proper and to language which was smooth and decorous. No doubt this showed that they were good citizens and good men, as indeed they were. It showed no less truly, however, that they either lacked

powerful poetical impulses or else misjudged the nature
of poetry, which to be memorable must be direct,
courageous, and ardent, and not merely graceful or ac-
ceptable to the majority. It has been claimed that the
scarcity of poets in the nineties was due about equally
to the exaggerated prestige of the older school and to
the exaggerated gentility of the newer school. Whatever the explanation, it is the fact that the last decade
of the century had, among many poets, few that are
now read or that deserve to be."

In "Petit the Poet," Edgar Lee Masters wrote the
epitaph of a whole shoal of versifiers who flourished in
the nineties, and Robinson himself, in his first volume,
eloquently voiced the need of his generation:

> Oh, for a poet—for a beacon bright
> To rift this changeless glimmer of dead gray;
> To spirit back the Muses, long astray,
> And flush Parnassus with a newer light;
> To put these little sonnet-men to flight
> Who fashion, in a shrewd mechanic way,
> Songs without souls, that flicker for a day,
> To vanish in irrevocable night.
> What does it mean, this barren age of ours?
> Here are the men, the women, and the flowers,
> The seasons and the sunset as before.
> What does it mean? Shall there not one arise
> To wrench one banner from the western skies,
> And mark it with his name forevermore?

"Songs without souls," that was the stuff of most of
the poetry that Robinson found around him when he
sent his own first book into the world. But at the same

time there was a more intense literary activity going on around him than these somber generalizations would indicate. Only by descending to the minutiæ of names and dates, can we suggest the literary landscape that the young poet found himself confronting.

In 1895, the year preceding that of "The Torrent and the Night Before," there was little native American poetry published that was worth a moment's notice; and the readers who knew where to look for better things turned to importations. Fresh from the press, among other collections, were Francis Thompson's "Sister Songs" and John Davidson's second series of "Fleet Street Eclogues." Fiona MacCleod's hybrid product of prose and poetry was winning wide favor, and "her" identity was still a fascinating mystery. In prose the real event of the year was undoubtedly the appearance of "Almayer's Folly," which was hailed by at least one organ of American criticism as "a serious and valuable contribution to literature," but it was Ian Maclaren's "Beside the Bonnie Brier Bush," and not Conrad's first novel, that was leading the ranks of the best-sellers. Kenneth Grahame's "The Golden Age" was charming the more discriminating readers of English on both sides of the Atlantic; and the popularity of Gyp in this country was emphasized by the issue of her latest story in four almost simultaneous translations. American readers who turned their eyes towards France saw the great name of Zola scrawled boldly across the horizon, and "naturalism" was the most vital of literary topics. From England word came, on good authority, that George Moore was to marry Mrs. Pearl

Craigie, better known as John Oliver Hobbes. Stephen Crane's "The Red Badge of Courage" was evoking irritated reviews from various critics before becoming a leading best-seller of 1896, and thereby sharing honors with such variegated works as Ian Maclaren's "Days of Auld Lang Syne," Harold Frederic's "The Damnation of Theron Ware," and John Kendrick Bangs' "A House-Boat on the Styx."

Robinson's first volume was printed in the same year that saw Howells come forward as a poet with "Stops of Various Quills." Guy Wetmore Carryl, Clinton Scollard, and Edith Thomas were all represented by published work. Paul Lawrence Dunbar was a lonely figure writing a generation in advance of the general literary awakening of his race. Lizette Woodworth Reese made her contribution to the year's poetic output with "A Quiet Road"; and "More Songs from Vagabondia" was greeted with popular applause. From England came Kipling's "The Seven Seas" and John Davidson's "New Ballads"; Paul Verlaine had died in France, Yeat's "Poems" had appeared, and an American edition of "A Shropshire Lad" was promised for the following year.

Aside from poetry there was much to keep the readers of 1896 extremely busy. The best-sellers already mentioned were being hard pressed by new books from the pens of Kate Douglas Wiggin, J. M. Barrie, F. Marion Crawford and Sarah Orne Jewett. Frank Stockton was at the height of his popularity, and "Sentimental Tommy" was running serially in *Scribner's*. "Quo Vadis" was taking the country by storm, and Stevenson's "Vailima Letters" were just out; Brander Matthews was writing novels, and Hamlin Garland had published "Rose of Dutcher's Coolly." In 1896 "Jude the Obscure" was shocking the conservative critics of two continents and eliciting such epithets as "degeneracy," "rottenness," and "filth." Sudermann's "Magda" appeared here in translation; Nathan Haskell Dole completed his long-heralded multi-variorum edition of the "Rubaiyat"; H. G. Wells was being hailed as a promising young writer; the reviewers were puzzling over Arthur Machen's "The Three Impostors"; it was stated that Richard Harding Davis would journey to Russia to witness the coronation of the Czar; and word came from England, on good authority, that George Moore would not marry Mrs. Pearl Craigie.

Even such brief bibliographical snippets as the above give some idea of the literary scene in the United States towards the close of the last century. Robinson made his debut in what we now retrospectively term a barren period, but this does not mean that the readers of that day were acutely aware of any sterility. A host of authors were clamoring for their favor, the presses were clanking busily, there was no lack of reading matter of all kinds. So it is in no way remarkable that Robinson's first work should have been overlooked by the majority of critics and readers. Rather it is remarkable that it should have been chosen for most favorable notice by the leading literary periodical of the day. Those who think of the youthful Robinson as a singer whose notes were heard by no one, may be surprised if they turn to *The Bookman* for February, 1897. There they may read:

"A little book of poetry containing some forty-four pages and bound in a plain sky blue paper cover, called *The Torrent and the Night Before*, has come to our table during the past month. It is printed by Messrs. Houghton, Mifflin and Company for the author, Mr. Edwin Arlington Robinson, whose address is Gardiner, Me., and is dedicated to 'Any man, woman, or critic who will cut the edges of it—I have done the top.' *The Torrent* begins

> I found a torrent falling in a glen
> Where the sun's light shone silvered and leaf split;
> The boom, the foam, and the mad flash of it
> All made a magic symphony; . . .

and those who read this and have any liking for poetry will read on to the end. Some of the verses we do not care for, especially the long poem at the end. There is true fire in his verse, and there are the swing and the singing of wind and wave and the passion of human emotion in his lines; but his limitations are vital. His humor is of a grim sort, and the world is not beautiful to him, but a prison-house. In the night-time there is weeping and sorrow, and joy does not come in the morning. But here and there in a sonnet he lets himself go, and the cry of a yearning spirit enters the lute of Orpheus and sounds a sweet and wondrous note. We quote one sonnet itself which is free and unstrained and spontaneous in its outburst, flinging itself into form with a natural *abandon* and full-blooded life:

> Oh, for a poet—for a beacon bright. . . ."

And then the reviewer quoted in its entirety the sonnet we have noted earlier.

Certainly the poet did not fare badly at the hands of his first critic: there were verses in the volume that Robinson himself soon ceased to "care for," and the "long poem at the end" was among them. Perhaps the most remarkable feature of this brief review is that it praises the poet for his "fire," "swing," "passion" and "abandon," qualities that later critics have rather ignored in their enraptured contemplation of "pure cerebration." But even more interesting than anything in the review itself is the reply that it elicited from the author criticized, for in this reply Edwin Arlington Robinson answered a host of his critics in advance, and at the same time furnished the key to what many have rather carelessly labeled his "pessimistic philosophy." The reply is editorially recorded in *The Bookman* for March, 1897:

"Mr. E. A. Robinson writes thanking us for 'the unexpected notice' of his book of poems called *The Torrent and the Night Before* in these columns in the February Bookman. Mr. Robinson adds: 'I am sorry to learn that I have painted myself in such lugubrious colors. The world is not a "prison-house," but a kind of spiritual kindergarten, where millions of bewildered infants are trying to spell God with the wrong blocks.' "

Here, at the very outset of his career, the poet has expressed more pungently and more succinctly than any critic might phrase it for him the view of life that he has sought constantly to express. In one brief sentence we find compacted the tragedy, the humor, the pity, and the doubt that are the vitalizing elements of Robinson's poetic utterance. Reduced to its simplest terms his poetical *corpus* is one great question to which he cannot presume to offer any answer. What is the meaning of life? Or is life worth the living? It is this interrogation, repeated times without number, that is the bourdon note of all his singing. Individual case after individual case he examines with sympathetic patience, constantly he searches his own soul and cons the faiths of all men for an answer, but judgment at the last must be withheld. And so he cannot reply to that lesser question which is but part of the greater one: What is success and what is failure? The apparent "failures" of the world obsess him, but constantly he repeats that he can pass no judgment. Within his spiritual kindergarten he will not presume to spell God, or any of God's patterns. But with the eternal patience of the philosopher he must constantly arrange and rearrange these blocks according to the inspirations of the artist. Some critics have claimed to trace a progress from "The Children of the Night" to "The Man Against the Sky"; they assert that the poet experienced a strengthening of faith during the years that lay between these two poems: but the progress and the strengthening really exist only in their own imaginations. The positive declaration of the former poem is as vigorous as that of the latter; the negative declaration of the latter is as darkly disturbing as that of the former. All who read "The Man Against the Sky" must perceive that the enduring question mark is still there; the poet has

advanced no further in his thinking than he had in
"Captain Craig" when, after stating two antithetical
views of life, he wrote

> Now the question is,
> Not which was right and which was wrong, for each
> By virtue of one-sidedness, was both;
> But rather—to my mind, as heretofore—
> Is it better to be blinded by the lights,
> Or by the shadows? By the lights, you say?
> The shadows are all devils, and the lights
> Gleam guiding and eternal? Very good;
> But while you say so do not quite forget
> That sunshine has a devil of its own,
> And one that we, for the great craft of him,
> But vaguely recognize.

As we consider the volumes that followed "The Children of the Night" we shall see that neither force in the
struggle between experience and faith could ever, for
long, claim any show of victory.

But the experience that breeds black pessimism in
many men did not at the first, and has not since, em-
bittered Robinson. Read once more that reply to the
charge that the world was for him a "prison-house,"
and you can never again mistake the man's character.
Much has been said of his "astringent humor," but we
must seek another adjective to fit the humor that he
reveals in "Mr. Flood's Party," let us say, and in a host
of other poems. Because of his pity he cannot be cruel,
and because of his humor he cannot be sentimental; his
scale is balanced well. He laughs at mankind, true; but

in his laughter there is no unkindly note. In "Isaac and Archibald" he has himself described his kind of laughter, and justified it once for all:

> Isaac and Archibald have gone their way
> To the silence of the loved and well-forgotten.
> I knew them, and I may have laughed at them;
> But there's a laughing that may have honor in it,
> And I have no regret for light words now.
> Rather I think sometimes they may have made
> Their sport of me;—but they would not do that,
> They were too old for that. They were old men,
> And I may laugh at them because I knew them.

Recording the "success of failure," as he does so often, there is small room for laughter of the bitter sort; and when he writes of failures that may well be judged complete, he does not laugh at all. For example, no smile flickered in his eyes when he wrote "Richard Cory," that popular and most readable of poems which no less an authority than Miss Lowell has called "more subtle, more ironical" than "John Evereldown"; and mention of which now calls for a slight discursion.

Some readers may have wondered at the bare mention of this poem when I was attempting to establish the quality of "The Children of the Night," and now is as good a time as any other to explain that the slight was intentional; for to me it seems so far below the higher levels of Robinson's accomplishment that when a critic, Mr. Clement Wood, whose opinion I usually respect, asserts that the poet has "never bettered the finish of 'Richard Cory,'" I can only marvel that one of us must be so irremediably wrong. Indeed, if this much too often quoted poem is to be quoted here, it shall be presented as displaying a kind of easy trickery that Robinson has consistently and triumphantly avoided; as depending upon a device that he might frequently have used, and which, to his credit, he has abjured. So here it is, in its entirety:

RICHARD CORY

Whenever Richard Cory went to town,
We people on the pavement looked at him;
He was a gentleman from sole to crown,
Clean favored and imperially slim.

And he was always quietly arrayed,
And he was always human when he talked,
But still he fluttered pulses when he said,
"Good morning," and he glittered when he walked.

And he was rich—yes, richer than a king—
And admirably schooled in every grace:
In fine, we thought that he was everything
To make us wish that we were in his place.

So on we worked and waited for the light,
And went without the meat and cursed the bread;
And Richard Cory, one calm summer night,
Went home and put a bullet through his head.

Now it might be argued that here Robinson comple-
ments his usual vision of the "success of failure" with
a glimpse of the "failure of success," and so far the
critic would be right. But "Richard Cory," viewed

in isolation, is no more than an anecdote depending upon a single point, put into neatly polished verse that glitters with a meretricious brilliance. The poem, like most anecdotes, is excellent, once. Both lose measurably in the retelling or the rereading, and that is not a fate which the best poetry shares with even the best anecdotes. The "finish," of which Mr. Wood has spoken in admiring terms, is no more than a snap of the whip, reminiscent of those curling flicks wherewith O. Henry was once wont to startle contemporary readers of short stories. Constructed solely for the sake of a single, final, startling line, the whole subservient poem must suffer once that line has lost its full effectiveness. The flick of the lash does not catch us off guard twice, and the time quickly comes when it falls short of reaching us at all.

Nowhere else has Robinson used this same device with equal blatancy, and his poetical fortunes have profited by his sagacity; it would have been so easy to turn the trick time and again in the field of compact tragic drama that he has made his own. There is some hint of a similar surprise in the last line of "Miniver Cheevy," but in that case what has gone before remains always intrinsically interesting, and is robbed of nothing in rereading. The concluding line merely adds a fillip to the whole character study, rather than toppling down a set of nine-pins that were set up only that they might be toppled. "Aaron Stark" and "Reuben Bright" are two more examples of how this element of surprise may be introduced at the last without sacrificing anything that has gone before; while such later and kindred poems as

"Bewick Finzer" demonstrate the complete and profitable rejection of this element. Place "Richard Cory" side by side with the latter, and then read them both. In the later portrait study every verse, every line, is interesting and valuable for its own sake, and at the same time the whole is bound together by an internal unity far stronger than any that might be given by a mere trick of construction. After reading the poem a score of times, we find that it has gained rather than lost; effectiveness of sense and sound have been augmented rather than impaired, and familiarity has bred in downright contradiction of the ancient adage. The precision of phrase employed is comparable to the precision of Pope; here, truly, is that "unapproachable technique" which Miss Lowell would generously attribute to specious ware; and if this same impeccable ease is sufficient to damn the poem and the poet in the eyes of certain critics who enjoy the spectacle of gestation rather more than that of final creative deliverance, some of us may value our own chosen spectacle all the more dearly for that very reason.

Contemplating a poem such as "Bewick Finzer," it is difficult to believe that the poet could have ever been charged with willful and malicious obscurity of thought and word; but there is an abundance in his work to explain, if not to justify, those very charges; and Robinson early courted such accusations. The greater part of "The Children of the Night" must have been clear as starlight to the readers of 1897, but there was another, smaller part that may well have lain in shadow for them. Browning had taught them that a poet may

plunge *in medias res,* and still emerge with his singing
robes cloaked decently about him; but Robinson, at the
very outset, began to experiment with an indirect,
oblique approach that has since become as character-
istic of him as his signature; a technique of poetic nar-
ration, description or dramatization not dissimilar to
the method that Conrad elaborated in prose. "Cliff
Klingenhagen" had its hint of mystery, and also "Fleming Hephelstine," while "The Story of the Ashes and
the Flame" foreshadowed such poems as "The Mill."
This poem, though it was written more than twenty
years later than those just mentioned, may well be
quoted here, for it is a perfect example of the technique
that has won its author a reputation for obscurity, and
without an understanding of this technique we cannot
profitably approach the body of his work.

THE MILL

The miller's wife had waited long,
And tea was cold, the fire was dead;
And there might yet be nothing wrong
In how he went and what he said:
"There are no millers any more,"
Was all that she had heard him say;
And he had lingered at the door
So long that it seemed yesterday.

Sick with a fear that had no form
She knew that she was there at last;
And in the mill there was a warm
And mealy fragrance of the past.

What else there was would only seem
To say again what he had meant;
And what was hanging from a beam
Would not have heeded where she went.

And if she thought it followed her,
She may have reasoned in the dark
That one of the few ways there were
Would hide her and would leave no mark;
Black water, smooth above the weir
Like starry velvet in the night,
Though ruffled once, would soon appear
The same as ever to the sight.

This tale of a miller who hanged himself to a beam
in his own mill, and of the wife who followed her husband to a suicide's grave, is typical of what Robinson
does with his material; and those who object offhand
to its obscurity should realize that it is, in great part,
to the indirect method that we owe the drama and the
haunting atmosphere which pervades the whole. Holding his subject in solution, as it were, the poet gains
the more powerful effect when he finally permits its
precipitation. Here, too, we see how poignantly he
makes use of under- rather than of over-statement.
"There are no millers any more," was all the wife had
heard her husband say, and in that single, simple sentence is summed up the tragedy of a class as well as an
individual. It is an unerring sense of values that permits a man to substitute one line of this sort for a dozen
lines he might have written; and with what restraint the
poet makes his major revelation:

"What else there was would only seem
To say again what he had meant. . . ."

Save for the one word that tells us the precise manner of his death, there is little, after that sure stroke, to be said of the miller's fate.

But we have spanned the years to show the final expression of what was only a tendency in 1897; for in writing of such a poet as Robinson it is impossible, or at least inadvisable, to attempt strict adherence to chronological order. He is constantly turning back upon himself, and if we would follow him we must more than once retrace our own steps to positions already familiar. Indeed, the critic's task is not so much to follow an advancing line as to circle steadily around a single central position, in the hope that his vision will be clarified as he sweeps closer and closer to his object.

III

OUR preliminary circlings have yielded considerable information as to both the substance and form of Robinson's utterance; we can unhesitatingly name the problem that obsesses him, and we have familiarized ourselves with the technique by which he translates that problem into poetry. So equipped, we may now consider as a single body of work the three volumes that followed "The Children of the Night." In certain instances the original editions of these books were augmented in later issues, but the precise dates of individual poems are not pertinent to our purpose. It is enough to know that "Captain Craig" was first published in 1902, "The Town Down the River" in 1910, and "The Man Against the Sky" in 1916. Neither in quality nor in ideational content are these three volumes essentially different from "The Three Taverns," 1920, and "Avon's Harvest," 1921. The group of five would prove as harmonious as the group of three; and "The Man Who Died Twice," 1924, might even make a sixth. But "The Children of the Night" and its immediate successors fall naturally together, while the others may logically be reserved for consideration after we have dealt with the long, major poems "Merlin" and "Lancelot." Where chronological order serves us well, there is no cause to flout it.

Of all Robinson's individual works, the title poem of

"Captain Craig" is undoubtedly the most neglected and the most maligned. Lloyd Morris in "The Poetry of Edwin Arlington Robinson" pays it no more heed than to give its name a passing mention; and those critics who have spoken of it at all have had little good to say of it. Miss Lowell found it "a dreary, philosophical ramble, occupying eighty-four pages, which, in spite of the excellent manipulation of its blank verse, reveals a fault which the earlier volume is conspicuously without, namely, verbosity. The one fault which has grown upon Mr. Robinson with the years is a tendency to long-windedness. There is an interminable amount of talking in 'Captain Craig,' and one must admit that the talking is both involved and dull." So far Miss Lowell. Mr. Louis Untermeyer bears witness: "For all its technical sprightliness and dialectic repartee, there is something a bit owlish in its unblinking seriousness, even in its irony. Captain Craig himself seems less a character-study than a peg on which to hang a great quantity of brilliant, sometimes beautiful but finally tiresome talk."

From all of which one would gather that "the Captain's tuneful ooze of rhetoric" is no more than "talk" deserving of no listeners. Yet we need only to turn to this poem, anywhere at random, to discover that much of its "talk" is poetry of the purest kind. And we discover more than this. Miss Lowell openly regrets that the old Captain was kept alive by the charity of four young men; but had he not been so cherished, we should have missed some of the most moving and most lucid of Mr. Robinson's philosophical statements. Nowhere has he attacked the central problem of his life and work with more directness, and nowhere has he translated his tentative answers into nobler poetry. If "Captain Craig" is wearisome to certain readers, it is not by reason of long-windedness, but because the verse is so tight-packed with thought and meaning that the reader's mind balks at the sustained effort which the poet would demand. Yet there are passages of singing words that are a balm to weariness, and those who deem the rest of the long journey valueless should find in these an ample compensation. That the poem lacks "artistic form" is not a pertinent criticism; it is undramatic in conception, and its form is in its very formlessness; it begins when the Captain begins talking, and it ends when he has said what he has had to say. His whim and purpose are the only arbiters of its length and structure.

The scheme of the poem is the simplest. Captain Craig is an ancient, unconsidered bit of flotsam that the waves of life have cast upon the inhospitable shores of Tilbury Town for his last, uneasy rest. He is a failure, and in his failure, even, there is nothing outwardly remarkable.

> I doubt if ten men in all Tilbury Town
> Had ever shaken hands with Captain Craig,
> Or called him by his name, or looked at him
> So curiously, or so concernedly,
> As they had looked at ashes; but a few—
> Say five or six of us—had found somehow
> The spark in him, and we had fanned it there,
> Choked under, like a jest in Holy Writ,
> By Tilbury prudence.

Which simply means that a small group of young men assumed responsibility for the Captain's continued existence, giving him the bare pittance that his life required. And after they "had laid some fuel to the spark of him, and oxidized it," they began to garner their reward (though Miss Lowell would give it another name), for in the Captain's words there came back more to them than they had ever given. He talks on and on, and when one of his benefactors goes away from Tilbury Town for a space, he writes on and on; and it is of his talking and his writing that the poem is composed. And such talk it is! It well repays the listening, for the outward "rhetoric" of it all is crowded deep with the essential elements of Robinson's thinking. Craig is a failure and may say

> "I who shape no songs of any sort,
> I who have made no music, thrilled no canvas,—
> I who have added nothing to the world
> The world would reckon save long-squandered wit—"

but he is, too, a humorist and a philosopher, and

> An irremediable cheerfulness
> Was in him and about the name of him. . . .

Let us listen for a space to the old Captain, discoursing like a king from the bottom of his one chair:

> ". . . . You have made
> The cement of your churches out of tears
> And ashes, and the fabric will not stand:
> The shifted walls that you have coaxed and shored

So long with unavailing compromise
Will crumble down to dust and blow away,
And younger dust will follow after them;
Though not the faintest or the farthest whirled
First atom of the least that ever flew
Shall be by man defrauded of the touch
God thrilled it with to make a dream for man
When Science was unborn.   And after time,
When we have earned our spiritual ears,
And art's commiseration of the truth
No longer glorifies the singing beast,
Or venerates the clinquant charlatan,—
Then shall at last come ringing through the sun,
Through time, through flesh, a music that is true.
For wisdom is that music, and all joy
That wisdom:—you may counterfeit, you think,
The burden of it in a thousand ways;
But as the bitterness that loads your tears
Makes Dead Sea swimming easy, so the gloom,
The penance, and the woeful pride you keep,
Makes bitterness your buoyance of the world.
And at the fairest and the frenziedest
Alike of your God-fearing festivals,
You so compound the truth to pamper fear
That in the doubtful surfeit of your faith
You clamor for the food that shadows eat.
You call it rapture or deliverance,—
Passion or exaltation, or what most
The moment needs, but your faint-heartedness
Lives in it yet: you quiver and you clutch
For something larger, something unfulfilled,
Some wiser kind of joy that you shall have
Never, until you learn to laugh with God."

This is the Captain's message, and those who cannot
see the poetry for the philosophy are beyond reach of

argument. Later I shall quote a passage of poetry
which can de denied by none; but first let us buttress
this solid quotation with another of its kind. The Captain reads his will:

"I, Captain Craig, abhorred iconoclast,
  Sage errant, favored of the Mysteries,
  And self-reputed humorist at large
  Do now, confessed of my world-worshiping,
  Time-questioning, sun-fearing, and heart-yielding,
  Approve and unreservedly devise
  To you and your assigns for evermore,
  God's universe and yours. If I had won
  What first I sought, I might have made you beam
  By giving less; but now I make you laugh
  By giving more than what had made you beam,
  And it is well. No man has ever done
  The deed of humor that God promises,
  But now and then we know tragedians
  Reform, and in denial too divine
  For sacrifice, too firm for ecstasy,
  Record in letters, or in books they write,
  What fragment of God's humor they have caught,
  What earnest of its rhythm; and I believe
  That I, in having somewhat recognized
  The formal measure of it, have endured
  The discord of infirmity no less
  Through fortune than by failure. What men lose,
  Man gains; and what man gains reports itself
  In losses we but vaguely deprecate,
  So they be not for us;—and this is right,
  Except that when the devil in the sun
  Misguides us we go darkly where the shine
  Misleads us, and we know not what we see:
  We know not if we climb or if we fall;
  And if we fly, we know not where we fly."

It would be pleasant and congruous to expand this quotation to include the succeeding passage, wherein the Captain inserts "an urging clause

> For climbers and up-fliers of all sorts,
> Cliff-climbers and high-fliers;"

but it is time to shift the emphasis from philosophy to poetry, from marshaled thoughts to wingèd words. Where shall we find a lovelier or more stirring passage than the following lines from this poem that so many critics would have us leave unread? Captain Craig is writing his first letter to the benefactor who has gone away from Tilbury Town:

> "I cannot think of anything to-day
> That I would rather do than be myself,
> Primevally alive, and have the sun
> Shine into me; for on a day like this,
> When chaff-parts of a man's adversities
> Are blown by quick spring breezes out of him—
> When even a flicker of wind that wakes no more
> Than a tuft of grass, or a few young yellow leaves,
> Comes like the falling of a prophet's breath
> On altar-flames rekindled of crushed embers,—
> Then do I feel, now do I feel, within me
> No dreariness, no grief, no discontent,
> No twinge of human envy."

Here, I submit, is something more than "excellent manipulation of blank verse," and I recommend it especially to those who insist that Robinson cannot throw off restraint, that his speech is always "cribbed, cabin'd and confined." That charge will be demolished later, but there is a certain satisfaction, not to be denied, in drawing at least one example from his least appreciated poem.

To demonstrate the variety of this same "Captain Craig," so frequently damned as monotonous, it might be well to quote the brief portrait it contains of "Count Pretzel von Würzburger, the Obscene," but perhaps another, feminine portrait, which graces the poem, will serve the purpose quite as well and more pleasantly. In it Mr. Untermeyer may find no more than "technical sprightliness"; but in my mind it need yield to a certain famous portrait of a wife of Bath on the grounds of antiquity only. In this instance the Captain quotes a friend who, as they were riding together, pointed out a woman to him, and remarked:

> "Now, you see,
> There goes a woman cursed with happiness:
> Beauty and wealth, health, horses,—everything
> That she could ask, or we could ask, is hers,
> Except an inward eye for the dim fact
> Of what this dark world is. The cleverness
> God gave her—or the devil—cautions her
> That she must keep the china cup of life
> Filled somehow, and she fills it—runs it over—
> Claps her white hands while some one does the sopping
> With fingers made, she thinks, for just that purpose,
> Giggles and eats and reads and goes to church,
> Makes pretty little penitential prayers,
> And has an eighteen-carat crucifix
> Wrapped up in chamois skin. She gives enough,
> You say; but what is giving like hers worth?
> What is a gift without the soul to guide it?
> 'Poor dears, and they have cancers?—Oh!' she says;

And away she works at that new altar-cloth
For the Reverend Hieronymus Mackintosh—
Third person, Jerry. 'Jerry,' she says, 'can say
Such lovely things, and make life seem so sweet!'
Jerry can drink, also.—And there she goes,
Like a whirlwind through an orchard in the spring-
    time—
Throwing herself away as if she thought
The world and the whole planetary circus
Were a flourish of apple-blossoms. Look at her!
And here is this infernal world of ours—
And hers, if only she might find it out—
Starving and sickening, suppurating,
Whirling to God knows where. . . . But look at her!"

Yes, look; but that is only half of it, for the woman
in turn describes the man, and doing so completes the
portrait of herself. And when both man and woman
have had their say, when we have had L'Allegro and Il
Penseroso in new forms, old Captain Craig comments
on both in the passage already quoted, which begins:

        "Now the question is,
Not which was right and which was wrong . . ."

Enough has been adduced here, I think, to demonstrate that "Captain Craig" is a poem well worth reading, and there I am content to let the matter rest. In
it the poet has treated at length a subject close akin to
many others that he has handled with dramatic brevity,
and in it he has most completely expressed his reiterated
conviction that judgment on a man's success or failure
cannot be passed by fellow men. For there may live

In ruin as in failure, the supreme
Fulfillment unexpressed, the rhythm of God
That beats unheard through songs of shattered men
Who dream but cannot sound it.

"Isaac and Archibald," the poem immediately succeeding "Captain Craig" in the 1902 volume, needs no
defense from any one. If anything, it has been over-
praised, for critics have aped one another in dismissing
the former poem briefly that they may pass on ad-
miringly to the later one. The explanation is not far
to seek. Where "Captain Craig" is tight-packed and
crowded with ideas, "Isaac and Archibald" is really
leisurely; and the result is that many persons find it
easy reading. One need only resign oneself to the gentle
flow of narrative; no mental gymnastics are called for.
So, too, the central idea is extremely simple and one
that exerts a sentimental rather than an intellectual
appeal. A young boy, through whose mouth the tale
is told, spends an afternoon with two old New Eng-
landers, and each, while ruminating much on youth and
age, confides to the youngster that he fears the other is
failing. The tender solicitude of each of the old men
for his ancient friend is undoubtedly responsible for
the wide popularity of the poem. In the main, it
is not made of the stuff of "Captain Craig," and its
beauties are earthly beauties; but there are some passages to which one returns again and again. In such
descriptions as the following, we find the best of it.
Archibald suggests that they go down cellar to test his
cider:

Down we went,
Out of the fiery sunshine to the gloom,
Grateful and half sepulchral, where we found
The barrels, like eight potent sentinels,
Close ranged along the wall. From one of them
A bright pine spile stuck out alluringly,
And on the black flat stone, just under it,
Glimmered a late-spilled proof that Archibald
Had spoken from unfeigned experience.
There was a fluted antique water-glass
Close by, and in it, prisoned, or at rest,
There was a cricket of the brown soft sort
That feeds on darkness. Isaac turned him out,
And touched him with his thumb to make him jump,
And then composedly pulled out the plug
With such a practiced hand that scarce a drop
Did even touch his fingers. Then he drank
And smacked his lips with a slow patronage
And looked along the line of barrels there
With a pride that may have been forgetfulness
That they were Archibald's and not his own.
"I never twist a spigot nowadays,"
He said, and raised his glass up to the light,
"But I thank God for orchards."

Such a passage shows to what homely ends a master
of blank verse may turn a meter framed expressly for
man's noblest emotions and most exalted moments; and
it shows, also, how such a master may achieve an almost colloquial ease without doing violence to the strict-
est requirements of his chosen form. The satisfaction
that this description gives is partially physical.

The other poems contained in the volume "Captain
Craig" are various in type and value. "Aunt Imogen"

is another character study done in subdued grays and gentle shadows; the portrait of the New England maiden aunt, sacrificed and sacrificing. "Saint-Nitouche" traces the complicated pattern of a man's spiritual experiences, concludes with a lamentably inadequate quatrain, and belongs to that large group of Robinson's poetry wherein judgment as to individual success or failure is withheld. "Erasmus" captures the spirit and the history of a man as well as such vast complications may be caught within the sonnet form; and "The Woman and the Wife" is notable for containing an epigrammatic expression of the commonplace conviction that is repeated many times, at greater length, throughout Robinson's writings:

> The dark is at the end of every day,
> And silence is the end of every song.

"The Corridor" shows the poet in one of his most cryptic moods: a lost opportunity is recorded, but the precise nature of that opportunity is an open subject for every reader's speculation. "Partnership" and "Twilight Song" are successful essays in more lilting meters than Robinson usually employs, and in "Variations on Greek Themes" he has amused himself by refashioning some of the lighter stuff of which the Anthology was made. "The Field of Glory" tells the tale of Levi, who toiled while other men made war, and who could find no reason for his own existence; but concerning his case as those of so many others, the poet characteristically concludes:

And who's of this and that estate
We do not wholly calculate,
When baffling shades that shift and cling
Are not without their glimmering;
When even Levi, tired of faith,
Beloved of none, forgot by many,
Dismissed as an inferior wraith,
Reborn may be as great as any.

By virtue of mere length alone, "The Book of Annandale" takes the third position of importance in this volume; but its real virtues are, in my opinion, confined almost entirely to the first half of the poem. The description of Annandale sitting alone in his room, after his wife's funeral, should be read by all who believe that Robinson is invariably indirect and barren of emotion. There are here an emotional depth and a simple directness of expression that could scarcely be surpassed:

For it had come at last, and she was gone
With all the vanished women of old time,—
And she was never coming back again.
Yes, they had buried her that afternoon,
Under the frozen leaves and the cold earth,
Under the leaves and snow. The flickering week,
The sharp and certain day, and the long drowse
Were over, and the man was left alone.
He knew the loss—therefore it puzzled him
That he should sit so long there as he did,
And bring the whole thing back—the love, the trust,
The pallor, the poor face, and the faint way
She last had looked at him—and yet not weep,
Or even choose to look about the room
To see how sad it was; and once or twice

He winked and pinched his eyes against the flame
And hoped there might be tears.

The story of Annandale's second marriage, after the
poem has shifted to the woman's point of view, is not so
well worth following: it takes a time for the reader to
orient himself after the sudden move the poet makes, it
is difficult for him to become interested in Damaris
after his preoccupation with Annandale, and the issues
of the drama lose themselves in vague confusion.

When we come to "The Town Down the River," which
begins with a remarkable interpretation of Lincoln and
ends with a nowise memorable tribute to Roosevelt, we
find no single poem that stands high above the rest, but
we do find good poetry in abundance and a dozen figures
or so to add to Robinson's gallery of failure-successes.
Leffingwell is one, Clavering a second; while "Exit" is
another plea that judgment be not passed upon the
dead, and "Alma Mater" records a sorry anonymous
human wreck. Lingard asks the old questions: Is life
worth living? Does anything come after? and receives
his answer from a rapping table:

"When earth is cold and there is no more sea,
There will be what was Lingard. Otherwise,
Why lure the race to ruin through the skies?
And why have Leffingwell, or Calverly?"—

Only a table speaking, but that is enough for one with
the will to believe; Lingard is content:

"I wish the ghost would give his name," said he,
And searching gratitude was in his eyes.

New England poetry, you will remember, began and
long continued in the elegiac strain; and Robinson is
a true New Englander in his determined contemplation
of death, however alien to the spirit of his forebears his
comments on the spectacle may be. It is surprising
how frequently his muse finds utterance in obituary
form; we have often noted the fact already, we shall
note it many times again.

Rounding out the tale of such poems that may be
found in "The Town Down the River," we make note
of "Pasa Thalassa Thalassa," "Leonora," "Bon Voyage," and "For a Dead Lady." The first, which records
the passing of an old sea-faring friend, is notable only
for its command of a meter familiar to all American
school-children; while the second may be reread for its
undulating, musical lines. "Bon Voyage" celebrates the
golden youth whose promise is unfulfilled:

> Child of a line accurst
> And old as Troy,
> Bringer of best and worst
> In wild alloy—
> Light, like a linnet first,
> He sang for joy.

"For a Dead Lady" should be lifted from amid the
many elegies that surround it, to be read in isolation,
for it is singularly lovely with a loveliness that Robinson has seldom essayed. The gracious notes fall lightly
on the ear with limpid purity:

The grace, divine, definitive,
Clings only as a faint forestalling;
The laugh that love could not forgive
Is hushed, and answers to no calling;
The forehead and the little ears
Have gone where Saturn keeps the years;
The breast where roses could not live
Has done with rising and with falling.

In "Atherton's Gambit" there is music, too, but there
is less clarity; it is a cryptic score the reader follows,
until he comes to the familiar close, that man shall not
pronounce judgment on his fellow man.

"Calverly's" really belongs among the elegies, for
here we read of an inn from which the spirit has de-
parted: the boon companions of old days are gone, the
familiar places are usurped by aliens, and no memory
of the old names lingers to haunt the hollow ruin.

Among the other poems in the 1910 volume there are
several that are memorable. "How Annandale Went
Out" brings us face to face with death again, but it is
a thing apart from the group dealt with above. The
theme is justified murder, and the poet-murderer con-
fesses only by implication. "They called it Annandale,"
the ruin on the bed; but the poet who was there had
known the man, and the contrast was unbearable.

Now view yourself as I was, on the spot—
With a slight kind of engine. Do you see?
Like this. . . . You wouldn't hang me? I thought not.

One thrust of the hypodermic needle, and the poignant
tragedy is over.

. "Miniver Cheevy" is perhaps the most widely known
and quoted of all Robinson's poems, so we need not
linger over it here. Readers who would fling "The
Mill" or "Cliff Klingenhagen" aside in despair, chant
with gusto:

> Miniver cursed the commonplace
> And eyed a khaki suit with loathing;
> He missed the medieval grace
> Of iron clothing

And the more critical realize how skillfully, in this
poem, Robinson has walked the almost invisible and
treacherous line that divides sly irony from downright
farce.

There are still other poems in "The Town Down the
River" that would repay consideration, did space per-
mit: the title poem, in which the familiar Robinsonian
questions are reiterated in a new pattern; "An Island,"
in which the soliloquizing Napoleon is plagued, on Saint
Helena, by a demon akin to one that plagues Rembrandt
in a later monologue; "Uncle Ananias," tribute to a
great and pleasant liar; "The Wise Brothers," wherein
optimism triumphs, although the way be lost; "Doctor
of Billiards" that tells of one who sacrificed his life to
become master of "three spheres of insidious ivory";
"Vickery's Mountain," the tale of a man sustained by
a dream he would never attempt to realize; and "The
White Lights," a hymn to Broadway which is glorified
by this first verse whose sounds break magnificently
upon the ear:

When in from Delos came the gold
That held the dream of Pericles,
When first Athenian ears were told
The tumult of Euripides,
When men met Aristophanes,
Who fledged them with immortal quills—
Here, where the time knew none of these,
There were some islands and some hills.

That a volume of the quality and variety of "The Town Down the River" should not have evoked immediate and wide critical applause is but a superfluous sad comment upon the perspicacity of every age. Robinson had another five or six years to wait before he was to receive the recognition that he had long deserved. Meantime, he was to write two prose plays, "Van Zorn" (1914) and "The Porcupine" (1915), which demand no more than mention in this study, for they are lone and comparatively unimportant excursions from the high-road of his life's effort, and they contain scant substance that has not been better fashioned within the limits of his own tempered medium. It would be simple to speculate upon the causes that impelled the poet to turn playwright: one might suggest that the cold reception of his accumulated work was responsible; and one might further hazard the opinion that once "Van Zorn" had been criticized as essentially undramatic, Robinson made a valiant effort to accommodate his genius to the laws of the theater. But, lacking definite information, we may assume with equal reason, and with greater charity, that these two plays were begotten by the creative spirit in a mood of sheer adventure.

The publication of "The Man Against the Sky," in 1916, marked the turning-point of Robinson's poetical fortunes. Before then, a few dispersed critics had noted the value of his work; and Theodore Roosevelt, who seems upon occasion to have had a shrewd eye for rising or risen genius, had so far appreciated the poet as to secure for him a position in the New York Custom House. But even this practical evidence of patronage, bestowed in 1905, had been of brief utility, for Robinson found that the writing of poetry precluded other occupation, and in 1909 he abandoned his one source of regular income. His discovery of the MacDowell Colony, in 1911, furnished him a haven where he might compose uninterruptedly through the summer months, and it is there that much of his later work has been accomplished.

Unquestionably it was great poetry, in "The Man Against the Sky," that awakened the critics and reviewers of the United States to the poet who had dwelt so long amongst them; but it was poetry no greater than Robinson had already written. As an integrated whole "Captain Craig" cannot bear comparison with the title poem in this later volume, but the best in the one is very nearly equal to the best in the other. "Ben Jonson Entertains a Man from Stratford," perfect as it is, merely demonstrated what the poet could accomplish in character depiction when he allowed himself more elbow-room than was his wont; in miniature he had turned the same trick a score of times before.

It has become fashionable for all who write of Robinson to quote the opening lines of the title poem in

"The Man Against the Sky," and if they are not quoted here no implied disparagement of their vaunted beauty is intended. They are beautiful, with a calm majesty that is unforgettable. But, since we are here concerned with ideas as well as poetry, I prefer to quote the closing lines, which suffer nowise in poetical comparison with the others, and which, it seems to me, have not been taken sufficiently into account by several of Robinson's critics. Miss Lowell has written: "We have only to compare this poem with 'The Children of the Night' to find how far Mr. Robinson has traveled, in twenty years, toward the peace which he is seeking. The bitterness of change is passing; in its stead, glimmers the dim hope of a new order." This seems, indeed, a strange judgment, when we recall the note of hope on which the early poem ended. Was it not—

> Let us, the Children of the Night,
> Put off the cloak that hides the scar!
> Let us be Children of the Light,
> And tell the ages what we are!

And the comparative judgment takes on an even stranger aspect when we place side by side with this earlier conclusion the close of "The Man Against the Sky." There we read

> If after all that we have lived and thought,
> All comes to Nought,—
> If there be nothing after Now
> And we be nothing anyhow,
> And we know that,—why live?
> 'Twere sure but weaklings' vain distress

> To suffer dungeons where so many doors
> Will open on the cold eternal shores
> That look sheer down
> To the dark tides of Nothingness
> Where all who know may drown.

Here is an almost negative conclusion, whereas the ending of the former poem was courageously affirmative. Of course, the implication is that our will to life, our faith in the purpose of continued existence, is such that we *do* live on instead of quietly exiting through one of the many doors available; but Robinson's fundamental question remains unanswered in this poem as in all the others. He simply shifts the burden of proof on to the shoulders of the professed pessimists, and observes that if they *know*, they have every opportunity to drown; but he knows that they do not know, any more than he, and nowhere in "The Man Against the Sky" does he lay claim to ultimate knowledge. And the best that he can offer, in the body of the poem, is his old, intuitive, mystical optimism that can never quite win the suffrage of reason:

> Where was he going, this man against the sky?
> You know not, nor do I.
> But this we know, if we know anything:
> That we may laugh and fight and sing
> And of our transience here make offering
> To an orient Word that will not be erased,
> Or, save in incommunicable gleams
> Too permanent for dreams,
> Be found or known.

Here is no expression of "the dim hope of a new order," but the familiar, defiant assertion that there *must* be a "Word" which is eternal, despite the failure of man's reason to discover it. For his own sustenance, Robinson has found it continually necessary to echo Eucken's dictum that life is greater than logic, and time and again he subscribes to the credo: *"Qu'est ce que la raison comprend? Presque rien: mais la foi embrasse l'infini."* But his sense of a truth transcending understanding has remained an intuition only; he has made no attempt to translate it into a metaphysical system, and consequently he has escaped a fate similar to that of Mr. Flosky, who, Peacock assures us, "plunged into the central opacity of Kantian metaphysics, and lay *perdu* for several years in transcendental darkness, till the common daylight of common sense became intolerable to his eyes."

Robinson's affirmative utterances are, rather than a "philosophy," the notes of one war-cry sounding clear amidst the tumult of his own internal struggle. But no more than he can we forget the opposing forces and their alien thunder. The hosts of darkness return to the charge again and again; it is the old unending conflict of Ahura Mazda and Agri Minos. In one of the most famous passages of "Ben Jonson Entertains a Man from Stratford," the poet has placed in Shakespeare's mouth the negation of all optimism, and it is significant that Robinson writes with equal conviction, equal power, as prolocutor for each of the opposing forces. His denial comes from the heart of his being,

as does his affirmation. Jonson describes to his Stratford visitor a recent encounter with Shakespeare:

> Not long ago, late in an afternoon,
> I came on him unseen down Lambeth way,
> And on my life I was afear'd of him:
> He gloomed and mumbled like a soul from Tophet,
> His hands behind him and his head bent solemn.
> "What is it now," said I,—"another woman?"
> That made him sorry for me, and he smiled.
> "No, Ben," he mused; "it's Nothing. It's all Nothing;
> We come, we go; and when we're done, we're done;
> Spiders and flies—we're mostly one or t'other—
> We come, we go; and when we're done, we're done."
> "By God, you sing that song as if you knew it!"
> Said I, by way of cheering him; "what ails ye?"
> "I think I must have come down here to think,"
> Says he to that, and pulls his little beard;
> "Your fly will serve as well as anybody,
> And what's his hour? He flies, and flies, and flies,
> And in his fly's mind has a brave appearance;
> And then your spider gets him in her net,
> And eats him out, and hangs him up to dry.
> That's nature, the kind mother of us all.
> And then your slattern housemaid swings her broom,
> And where's your spider? And that's Nature, also.
> It's Nature, and it's Nothing. It's all Nothing.
> It's all a world where bugs and emperors
> Go singularly back to the same dust,
> Each in his time; and the old, ordered stars
> That sang together, Ben, will sing the same
> Old stave to-morrow."

And in the face of this, stout old Ben can think of no
better remedy than a "grateful nook" where Will can
drink:

He'll drink, for love of me, and then be sick;
A sad sign always in a man of parts,
And always very ominous.

The artist Shakespeare distresses learned Jonson almost as much as does the man in his despondent moods, and this distress is phrased by Robinson in poetry forever memorable:

He's all at odds with all the unities,
And what's yet worse, it doesn't seem to matter;
He treads along through Time's old wilderness
As if the tramp of all the centuries
Had left no roads—and there are none, for him;
He doesn't see them, even with those eyes,—
And that's a pity, or I say it is.

But even the man of Aristotle knows genius when he sees it, and the words that Robinson lends to him compose as fine an appreciation of unhampered creative effort as ever has been penned:

For granted once the old way of Apollo
Sings in a man, he may then, if he's able,
Strike unafraid whatever strings he will
Upon the last and wildest of new lyres;
Nor out of his new magic, though it hymn
The shrieks of dungeoned hell, shall he create
A madness or a gloom, to shut quite out
A cleaving daylight, and a last great calm
Triumphant over shipwreck and all storms.
He might have given Aristotle creeps,
But surely would have given him his *katharsis*.

There is no doubt that "Ben Jonson Entertains a Man from Stratford" is as flawless a poem as Robinson has given us, and one of the most stimulating. It was a canny art that gave vitality to the immortal, legendary Shakespeare by throwing into relief the one petty human aspiration that his most trustworthy biographers record: all his London triumphs were small beer compared to the one triumph that he sought, to build his house upon the Avon and stroll among his fellow-townsmen as the Duke of Stratford. In Robinson's creation it is the man's humanity that sets off his divinity; we have an earth-mark whereby to calculate his soaring flight.

There are no other poems in this same volume to match with the two we have considered; but there is good poetry in abundance. "John Gorham," a dialogue in ballad form, is a remarkable achievement in that the writer conveys the impression of colloquial New England conversation while actually employing an idiom that is decidedly poetic. To read this poem many times is steadily to increase one's liking for it; the old, old scene of lovers parting is shrouded in an atmosphere that is peculiarly Robinson's own. John Gorham has come to say good-by forever to Jane Wayland, and she has protested lightly so far as pride permits her to protest. At the last her tone grows graver, but the man is obdurate:

"Won't you ever see me as I am, John Gorham,
  Leaving out the foolishness and all I never meant?
  Somewhere in me there's a woman, if you know the way
    to find her.
  Will you like me any better if I prove it and re-
    pent?"—

"I doubt if I shall ever have the time, Jane Wayland;
  I dare say all this moonlight lying round us might as
    well
Fall for nothing on the shards of broken urns that are
    forgotten
As on two that have no longer much of anything to
    tell."

"The Clinging Vine" records another parting, more rapidly articulate, in which the woman has the last word. Matching the close of the preceding poem with the conclusion of this one is an interesting comparison in technique.

> "My burden? You would share it?
>   Forbid the sacrifice!
> Forget so quaint a notion,
>   And let no more be told;
> For moon and stars and ocean
>   And you and I are cold."

"Flammonde" and "The Poor Relation" are worthy additions to the portrait gallery that Robinson is constantly enriching. "The man Flammonde, from God knows where," is himself a kind of failure, a "Prince of Castaways," a mystery to Tilbury Town; but he mends the destinies of others, although unable to direct his own, and when he passes from the scene the folk of Tilbury Town scan the horizons for his possible return. Here we have the same precise, etched phrases that we note in "Bewick Finzer" and "Miniver Cheevy."

> Erect, with his alert repose
> About him, and about his clothes,

He pictured all tradition hears
Of what we owe to fifty years.
His cleansing heritage of taste
Paraded neither want nor waste;
And what he needed for his fee
To live, he borrowed graciously.

"The Poor Relation" fulfills the promise of the title. The lonely woman lives on the empty charity that blood-relationship assures her, apologizing the while for her existence. Her visitors, who come impelled by duty, leave so soon as they have done "What penance or the past requires," and she is left "To count her chimneys and her spires," and to wear and mend "The poor relation's odds and ends."

The other poems of this collection are various, and if they are only mentioned here it is no sign that several of them are not deserving of more extended treatment. "Eros Turannos" is haunting and suggestive, with a magnificent last verse. "Stafford's Cabin" is the sort of mysterious tale that Robinson loves to tell, with the essential clew omitted. "Cassandra" voices a prophetic warning to America, foreshadowing the later, elaborated utterance of "Dionysus in Doubt." In "The Gift of God" the poet turns the light of gentle irony upon exaggerated mother-love; and in "Veteran Sirens" he escapes banal sentiment by the saving grace of a flawless technique. "Bokardo" is a monologue, wherein the speaker offers forgiveness and consolation, not unbarbed with irony, to a friend who has wronged him. "Old King Cole" expresses a resignation to the ills of life, and a joy in its simple pleasures, that approaches sage indifference. "Old Trails" introduces us to the failure of success instead of the familiar success of failure. With "Llewellyn and the Tree" before us, we see where Robinson's humor might have led him had he always granted its exuberance free play; every touch is light, every stroke is sure. Llewellyn would have been the best of husbands.

> But howsoever mild he was
>   Priscilla was implacable;
> And whatsoever timid hopes
>   He built—she found them, and they fell.

But Priscilla did not quite know her man, and before eight more verses have passed by:

> One gold October afternoon
>   Great fury smote the silent air;
> And then Llewellyn leapt and fled
>   Like one with hornets in his hair.

He did not flee alone, nor did he return; his repression had been released at last by another's touch, by woman who tossed roses in his path,

> Though many made no more of her
>   Than civet, coral, rouge, and years.

There is no need to pursue the tale so far as the moral, enunciated by Llewellyn many years after his hejira; every reader may follow easily for himself the lilting trail of verse.

With Llewellyn we take leave of "The Town Down

the River," but in going I would borrow for a moment from Mr. Louis Untermeyer. I cannot agree with him that "Llewellyn and the Tree" is a "Freudian analysis of repressed desire,"—it is something far less pretentious and depends upon a simple knowledge of human nature that is older than Freud; but I do agree with the following passage, and prefer to quote it rather than weaken it by paraphrase.

"In this volume we notice with greater emphasis how strict and simple are the forms Robinson uses and how much he is at home in them. Even the rhyme-schemes are free of any twist or innovation. He takes patterns that are severe and anything but original and, without an effort to change the shape, makes them somehow his own. In fact, some of the most intense and serious things he has written are cast in the identical light-verse stanzas of Austin Dobson, C. S. Calverly and Locker-Lampson. These poems are, in themselves, a complete refutation of the still persisting theory that nothing psychological, nothing probing or intimately sensitive— in short, that nothing 'new'—can be expressed in the old forms (vide Mr. Edward Storer), that rhyme and a regular rhythm will, in a few years, be practically obsolete. Such brilliant and analytic verse as Robinson's completely explodes the fallacy that (I quote Mr. Storer's conclusion) 'a poet who wishes to give expression to realities in modern life . . . will find that he is confined for his literary expression to the two media of prose and free verse.' Page after page in this collection refutes this exceedingly impressionistic dictum."

Robinson wrote steadily through the period of our

little poetic rebellion, oblivious to the battle-cries and manifestos of the insurgent camps; and it is significant that the most gifted rebels of 1914 have long since done voluntary service in the court of the immortal and exceedingly conservative Muses. "For granted once the old way of Apollo, sings in a man," he may strike what strings he will "Upon the last and wildest of new lyres," but he may also, and with equal profit, as Edwin Arlington Robinson has so amply shown, "strike unafraid" whatever strings he will upon old lyres, and by his magic striking prove them ever new.

IV

WHEN we reach the long poem "Merlin," which was published in 1917, we find ourselves again on hotly controversial ground. Miss Margaret Wilkinson tells us: "It is unsuccessful because Mr. Robinson has not the temperament for that task. He can think back into the period when men believed in wizardry, but he cannot feel the period and vitalize it." Mr. Untermeyer considers it an "interval book" and asserts: "Robinson has written all around the Arthurian romance; he has invested it with gorgeous color and a flashing vocabulary; his alert mentality plays through it and transforms it into something extraordinarily complex. He does everything to it, in fact, except vitalize it." And Miss Lowell, despite the haunting, inevitable conclusion of the poem, which she herself quotes, was able to write: "A work of art should round its pattern somehow. 'Merlin' fails to satisfy because the ends ravel away without any such rounding."

Were these judgments the expressions of critics who lacked all admiration for Robinson's work, it would be impertinent to quote them here; but coming from such sources as they do, they provoke, indeed demand, a downright contradiction. I not only believe that the poet has succeeded in vitalizing the Arthurian legend, but also that the poem "Merlin" is instinct with a dual vitality: the characters possess the life of epic figures, with all their grandeur and their mystery, and the life of modern individuals, with all their psychological and emotional complexities. It is by virtue of this rare synthesis that Robinson's achievement in this poem, and in "Lancelot" (1920), is so remarkable; had he sacrificed the epic character to modernity, or modernity to the epic character, his accomplishment would have been diminished by one-half. As it is, he has made unique his handling of an old, old theme. Indeed, I am convinced that he is the only man since Malory who has succeeded in endowing this particular group of lengendary characters with life; beside his figures, those of Tennyson are pale phantoms gliding over lawns of dreamland. And so he has amply justified what always requires justification: the retelling of an ancient story that has been well told many times before. Beneath his touch, the immortal tale is again reborn; the tale that drifted down from the north country into Wales, that wandering singers carried out of Wales to Brittany, and thence to France, and back from France again into the British Isles, where poets ever since have known its haunting inspiration.

There are critics who find in "Merlin" and in "Lancelot" a poet's response to the impact of the world war; and Lloyd Morris, asserting that they were written under this influence, tells us "they are therefore necessarily pictures of a world in solution." When criticism goes hunting symbolism and allegory—the medieval critic's favorite quest—the chase is often interesting, but the quarry seldom offers adequate compensation for the run that has carried us far from an appreciation of poetry as poetry, and led us to a discovery of its dubious value as something else. To be sure, it is a world in solution that we find pictured in these poems, but I prefer to believe that it is an older world than that which trembled when gray-clad troops swept like a flood upon Liége; I prefer to read its geography without symbolism, to believe utterly in the reality— and, for poetry, complete adequacy—of Camelot, Broceliande, and Joyous Gard. Certainly the events witnessed in his own lifetime have enabled Robinson to understand and to describe the doom of Camelot with the vividness and poignancy of fate experienced; but for me it is pleasanter to think that he has brought his knowledge of the present to an illumination of the Arthurian legend, rather than that he pressed eternal figures into the service of a studied symbolism. Arthur and Lancelot, Merlin and Vivian, Gareth and Guinevere, are more alive in these poems than symbols have a right to be. Reading of them, let us read of them for their own sakes.

Having begun to write of "Merlin" alone, I find that "Merlin" and "Lancelot" have become inextricably interwoven during the few preceding paragraphs, and it is well that they should be, for they may best be treated as units of a single whole. Three years elapsed between their publication dates, but the critical reader is conscious of no separating gulf; for together they really form one long, tragic poem. "Merlin" prepares us for tragedy, "Lancelot" plunges us into the tragedy itself; the magnificent close of the earlier poem is but the prelude to a conclusion that is absolute in its finality.

When Merlin takes his last leave of Arthur and his
court, knowing that no wisdom of his, nor any wisdom
upon earth, can stay the march of fate, the doom of
Camelot is plain to read; thenceforward the progress of
events is merciless. The seer, and Dagonet the fool,
turn their faces from a city and a man they both have
loved:

> They arose,
> And, saying nothing, found a groping way
> Down through the gloom together. Fiercer now,
> The wind was like a flying animal
> That beat the two of them incessantly
> With icy wings, and bit them as they went.
> The rock above them was an empty place
> Where neither seer nor fool should view again
> The stricken city. Colder blew the wind
> Across the world, and on it heavier lay
> The shadow and the burden of the night;
> And there was darkness over Camelot.

Few poems can show a more powerfully decisive
ending; when Merlin and the fool groped through the
gloom, it was the end of Merlin's wisdom and the end
of that most earthly seer who had wooed oblivion in a
woman's arms; but it was not yet the end of Camelot
and Arthur's world, however unmistakable the portents.
Nor had the final acts of an illicit, fateful love yet been
played out. Arthur still lived, and Lancelot and
Guinevere had still to hold their last sad empty speech
at Almesbury. "Lancelot" records the ending of a
world, the ending of an age, the age of chivalry; and
this poem is not merely a sequel to, but one with, "Merlin."

In my opinion this single lengthy blank verse narrative contains two of the most moving love stories in English poetry; and I am convinced that the reader who will best appreciate "Merlin" and "Lancelot," and carry away the most of what the poet put into them, is the one who will read them, not for their philosophy or symbolism, but for the sake of these two immortal stories. The guilty love of Lancelot for Guinevere, and the fateful love of Merlin for Vivian, have found in Robinson their greatest troubador. An intellectual bard he is, to be sure, and not one to shy at psychological subtleties; but he is, too, a passionate singer able to animate old themes with a burning vitality. He can lift a human drama to the heights without draining from it one drop of its humanity. Let those who call him cold, aloof, and bloodless, read this passage from the long description of Merlin's first evening with Vivian at Broceliande. The two are just about to sup together; Vivian in a crimson gown, and Merlin shorn of his beard.

"Yes, you are like a tree,—or like a flower;
More like a flower to-night." He bowed his head
And kissed the ten small fingers he was holding,
As calmly as if each had been a son;
Although his heart was leaping and his eyes
Had sight for nothing save a swimming crimson
Between two glimmering arms. "More like a flower
To-night," he said, as now he scanned again
The immemorial meaning of her face
And drew it nearer to his eyes. It seemed
A flower of wonder with a crimson stem
Came leaning slowly and regretfully

To meet his will—a flower of change and peril
That had a clinging blossom of warm olive
Half stifled with a tyranny of black,
And held the wayward fragrance of a rose
Made woman by delirious alchemy.
She raised her face and yoked his willing neck
With half her weight; and with hot lips that left
The world with only one philosophy
For Merlin or for Anaxagoras,
Called his to meet them and in one long hush
Of capture to surrender and make hers
The last of anything that might remain
Of what was now their beardless wizardry.
Then slowly she began to push herself
Away, and slowly Merlin let her go
As far from him as his outreaching hands
Could hold her fingers while his eyes had all
The beauty of the woodland and the world
Before him in the firelight, like a nymph
Of cities, or a queen a little weary
Of inland stillness and immortal trees.

Or let those who find no warmth in Robinson's descriptions—those who think of his protagonists as making intellectual patterns in a colorless void—read of Merlin sitting down to sup,

With Vivian's inextinguishable eyes
Between two shining silver candlesticks
That lifted each a trembling flame to make
The rest of her a dusky loveliness
Against a bank of shadow.

Or let them read how,

With a long-kindling gaze that caught from hers
A laughing flame, and with a hand that shook
Like Arthur's kingdom, Merlin slowly raised
A golden cup that for a golden moment
Was twinned in air with hers; and Vivian,
Who smiled at him across their gleaming rims,
From eyes that made a fuel of the night
Surrounding her, shot glory over gold
At Merlin, while their cups touched and his trembled.

There is, indeed, an almost barbaric splendor in this part of "Merlin," a lavish sensuous beauty and a rich sensual passion that incarnate the dreams of no merely "cerebral" poet. This time, at least, Robinson has completely "let himself go," and the result is magnificent. Then the glory fades, from the poet's eyes as from the eyes of Vivian and Merlin, and we hear a misunderstood man asking a misunderstanding woman:

"Why does a woman,
Made otherwise a miracle of love
And loveliness, and of immortal beauty,
Tear one word by the roots out of a thousand
And worry it, and torture it, and shake it,
Like a small dog that has a rag to play with?
What coil of an ingenious destiny
Is this that makes of what I never meant
A meaning as remote as hell from heaven?"

Now we find ourselves amid familiar twists of language that are admittedly "Robinsonian," but he who cannot hear the throttled passion in these words must be deaf save to his own voice. And what of the emotion with which the following passage of farewell is alive?

No more will Merlin's glass be "twinned in air" with
Vivian's; and he is speaking:

"I saw too much when I saw Camelot;
And I saw farther backward into Time,
And forward, than a man may see and live,
When I made Arthur king. I saw too far,
But not so far as this. Fate played with me
As I have played with Time; and Time, like me,
Being less than Fate, will have on me his vengeance.
On Fate there is no vengeance, even for God."
He drew her slowly into his embrace
And held her there, but when he kissed her lips
They were as cold as leaves and had no answer;
For Time had given him then, to prove his words,
A frozen moment of a woman's life.

These quotations might be buttressed by a dozen or
more from "Lancelot," in which the emotional currents
are no less intense. From the conversation between
Lancelot and Guinevere in the King's garden, with which
the poem opens, we might lift a hundred lines whereof
each syllable is animated by a human breath; or, from
the body of the narrative, we could take the picture of
the King, alone with Gawaine, torturing himself with
the image of the guilty pair speeding

To Joyous Gard, where Tristram and Isolt
Had islanded of old their stolen love. . . .

And then there are two other scenes that would serve
our purpose quite as well, or better: Lancelot, telling
the Queen she must go back to Camelot; and that amaz-
ing, final interview at Almesbury. But the dismember-

ment occasioned by quotation is a sorry business and may, if carried to incautious lengths, defeat the ends of him who practices it.

I have dwelt at such length upon the purely emotional elements in "Merlin" and in "Lancelot" for the simple reason that Robinson is usually written of as an unemotional poet. We have heard too much of the man's astringent irony, of his cold detachment, and his cerebral complexity; too much of his philosophy, and his precise psychological patterns. Such descriptive terms are accurate enough, but they describe the poet by half, and only half his work. There is another Robinson, who has been ignored by the critics; and the fullness of his expression may be found in the tales of Guinevere and Lancelot, of Vivian and Merlin. His voice is heard fleetingly in the earlier poems, infusing them with life and human poignancy; but in these two it is dominant, and for that reason they are, I think, the greatest of all his creations. In them the balance of the heart and mind is perfect. He has not thought "himself back into the period when men believed in wizardry." He has brought the legendary figures of Camelot forward into the living present, and made them one with the men and women of all time. Although he shares none of Miniver's illusions regarding "iron clothing," the world of Arthur has furnished him with his most congenial theme and has called forth all his powers. Perhaps he may find another like it, but he has not found it yet.

Indeed, the poems that have appeared since "Lancelot" may be dealt with more briefly than any of their predecessors; not because they represent a general decline in power, but because they show no notable growth or variation in method and ideas. Two may be set apart from their fellows: the title poem of "Dionysus in Doubt," as a comparative failure; and "Rembrandt to Rembrandt," as an unqualified success that cannot be accurately paralleled in Robinson's earlier work. But consideration of these should be postponed in favor of another, longer work that may be set side by side with "Merlin" and "Lancelot."

"Roman Bartholow" was published in 1923. It consists of four thousand and some hundreds of blank verse lines. In it the poet had all the room that he allowed himself in his Arthurian stories, and he had an analogous subject; but he could not quite raise his characters to the stature required of them. Here is an interesting paradox: the half-shadowy folk of far-off Camelot aroused and interested him intensely as men and women; the supposedly contemporary figures of Bartholow, Gabrielle, Penn-Raven, and Umfraville seem to exist in his mind's eye only as factors in a human problem, and he handles them much as one might finger the pieces on a mysterious chess board that called for moves one did not wholly understand. The directing player seems bent upon discovery through experiment; the atmosphere of mystery remains, to the last, undispelled.

Certain essential outlines clarify themselves, of course: Bartholow is suffering from some undefined spiritual malady, and he is cured by his friend Penn-Raven, who steals away the patient's wife the while he practices his therapeutic art; Gabrielle's confession is followed by her suicide, and it is left for the fantastic scholar-fisherman, Umfraville, to nurse Bartholow back to a new life. But Penn-Raven marches swathed in shadows thicker than any that ever hid Merlin's wisdom from the world, while Bartholow and Gabrielle are illumined by no such sun as beat upon the brows of Vivian and Arthur. As for Umfraville, make of him what you will. Perhaps he is blood-brother to Flammonde, a man who can straighten all warped destinies except his own; perhaps he is a grotesque and late-begotten child of the old Greek tragic chorus. In either case, he is a gray figure in a misty world, as are the two men and the fated woman whose lives afford him matter for contemplation and sage comment.

However, there are passages here that are comparable to the best in "Lancelot," although such passages are briefer and fewer than in the earlier poem. There is intensity, though it is intellectualized; there are many lines of thoughtful beauty, and there is the growth within an organic whole that is the process of true art. In "Roman Bartholow" the poet undoubtedly repeats what he has said many times before. We read,

> "All this will end,"
> He thought, in the old way of all who think
> Too little and too late; "and when all this
> Is ended, the same moon will shine again
> As it shines now, and over the same river.
> The river and the moonlight and the trees,
> When I am gone, will be as when I came—"

and we find it no improvement upon that superb pas-

sage in "Ben Jonson Entertains a Man from Stratford," which ends,

> "It's all a world where bugs and emperors
> Go singularly back to the same dust,
> Each in his time; and the old, ordered stars
> That sang together, Ben, will sing the same
> Old stave to-morrow."

But we do find it a new and lovely phrasing of the old
refrain; and what fecund artist of the first rank is there
who has not repeated himself, to the greater joy and
benefit of all his readers?

Technically, at least, I fail to discover in this poem
the running to seed that one critic has noted. As to the
charge that its blank verse descends at time to arid
prose, I should rather say that it declines at times from
glorious to inferior verse, as does the verse of Milton,
Marlowe and Shakespeare, as does the verse of every
great poet who has ever written in this meter which is
so perfectly adapted to man's supreme hours of thought
and action, and so ill adapted to his lesser moments.
Mr. Robinson is writing in the meter which, since Surrey
was inspired to translate the fourth Æneid into unrhymed decasyllables, has been considered the fittest
poetic form for the expression of heroic movement and
lofty sentiment. This has been called the easiest of all
meters to write, and the most difficult to write well. It
is a meter that requires continual departures from strict
regularity to render it tolerable to the sensitive ear;
unrelieved by an occasional pyrrhic, by a not infrequent
spondee, by the welcome superfluous unaccented syllable

of the feminine ending, unrhymed iambic pentameter becomes too monotonous to give pleasure. Mr. Robinson manipulates this meter with the sureness and flexibility of a master; he makes his rhythm a living, growing thing, rather than the exact reiteration of a precise recurrence. By his liberties, you may know him. "Theophrastus," you may remember, "was discovered not to be a native of Athens, by so strict an adherence to the Attic dialect, as shewed that he had learned it not by custom, but by rule." The author of "Roman Bartholow" courts no such discovery.

Emphatically it may be repeated that he does not descend to prose; but he is writing in what is rightly called "English heroic blank verse," and at times his material is too trivial for the grandest of English meters. Usually his medium is admirably adapted to his needs,—and in the Arthurian tales it is inevitable; but when, for example, he describes a modern breakfast, the light freight rattles in the capacious vehicle, and he must summon to his aid the dubious padding of circumlocution to hold his load in place. However, let us not forget that even greater poets than Edwin Arlington Robinson have been troubled, when using this meter, by trivialities analogous to this breakfast scene, and that they have been forced, as he has been, to levels far below their highest flights.

Of "The Man Who Died Twice," 1924, I shall say little. As stated earlier, it fits unobtrusively into a large group of Robinson's poems; and, frankly, it is his only composition of any length to which I am totally indifferent. Perhaps it does not, as a whole, fall below his average level, but it never rises, as the other poems do in parts at least, above it. The story of Fernando Nash is the competent work of a practiced artist employing a tested medium. The elements are all familiar, we know their magic properties when they are cunningly combined; but somehow, in this case, they contribute only to a laboratory experiment. There is no miracle.

Fernando Nash, for all the twelve hundred odd lines devoted to him, never captures our imagination,—or mine at least. A sonnet might have turned the trick; but that is speculation. Only indifference can be proffered here, as a sorry substitute for criticism. Yet a statement of indifference is critical comment of a kind, and that is all the comment I can make upon this tale of one more Robinsonian failure: a man who was born, it seemed, to write great symphonies; who went down to Hell, and who returned to beat the drum of salvation amidst

> The caps and bonnets of a singing group
> That loudly fought for souls. . . .

"Dionysus in Doubt," which appeared in 1925, is another matter; and no indifference shall record it here. Between the first poem and the last—companion pieces—there are memorable sonnets in the best manner of an accomplished sonneteer; there is a dialogue neatly turned; and there is "Mortmain," which should be granted a place among the minor masterpieces of a master of blank verse. But "Dionysus in Doubt" and "Demos and Dionysus,"—that first poem and that last? Despite all prejudice in favor of their author, despite all predilection and all love, I could wish most heartily that they had died still-born.

Matthew Arnold insisted in his solid way that poetry should be a criticism of life, and these two poems answer with a vengeance to his test, for they are, generally speaking, a criticism of democracy as it is practiced all around us; more particularly, a criticism of current legislation; and, even more especially, a criticism of the Eighteenth Amendment to the Constitution of the United States. It would be folly to object that Mr. Robinson's chosen subject is unpoetical; such subjects must remain undefined until the last unwritten poem of all the yet unborn poets has taken form in words. And I am certainly in full agreement with Mr. Robinson's criticism of democracy in general, as well as with his criticism of the Eighteenth Amendment in particular. My quarrel with him rests on no such grounds as these. Like him, I can find no joy in the prophecy of Demos:

> The waste of excellence that you call art
> Will be a thing remembered as a toy
> Dug somewhere from forgotten history;
> And this infirmity that you name love
> Will be subdued to studious procreation.

And Dionysus has my heartiest approval when, in no uncertain terms, he informs the spirit of democracy:

I mean that your delirious clumsy leap
From reason to the folly you call reason
Will only make of you and of your dupes
A dislocated and unlovely mess
For undertakers, who are not yet born
To view the coming ruin that is to be
Their occupation and emolument—
If your delusion for a time prevail
As like enough it will.

With the sense and sentiment of all these words, few
sanely thoughtful men will take issue. Let Demos be
assigned the rôle of villain; it is just. But we demand
of a true poet something more than satiric tracts in
verse, however keen their edge may prove; and when
he chooses to speak with the voice of a great god's son,
we may expect him to put into that august, wine-stained
mouth words that have qualities to recommend them
other than those of simple common sense.

There, briefly, is my argument: that a true poet has,
on one occasion, failed to make poetry of his chosen
matter. But happily this volume has a middle, as well
as a beginning and an end; and in that middle section
there is much to praise. In "Mortmain" we find a subject and characters of the kind with which Robinson
is always peculiarly successful. Avenal Gray and
Seneca Sprague, and the final scene of their long court-
ship, furnish him matter fit for his original act of
transmutation. Seneca has wooed Avenal for thirty
years or more, but the woman remains faithful to the
memory of her brother, as she remained faithful to him
during his lifetime. Seneca comes to her garden to
make his final plea; and after he has spoken:

He watched her face and waited, but she gave him
Only a baffled glance before there fell
So great a silence there among the flowers
That even their fragrance had almost a sound. . . .

Reading these lines, we may forget such journalistic
jargon as Dionysus utters when he speaks of severities
calculated

To moronize the million for the few.

And as an added aid to forgetfulness there are the sonnets. "A Man in Our Town," reminiscent of "Flammonde"; "Haunted House," with the effective weirdness
that Robinson so frequently achieves; "The Sheaves,"
with those beautiful closing lines, so often quoted since
the sonnet's publication.

Who was the Frenchman who always tore from a book
only those leaves that he enjoyed, consigning the re-
mainder to the flames? He was a vandal certainly, but
on occasion pardonable. Let me repeat, "Dionysus in
Doubt" has a middle, as well as a beginning and an end.

It may be that sentimental reasons have dictated my
departure from strict chronology towards the conclusion of this study, that I did not wish to close in
accents of dispraise this consideration of a poet whom
I so heartily admire. At all events, "The Three
Taverns," 1920, and "Avon's Harvest," 1921, still
await our scrutiny. What do we find in them?

We find, I think, in these two volumes, precisely one
poem that commands our attention after this fairly

lengthy, if somewhat superficial, journey through Edwin Arlington Robinson's poetic world. Do not mistake me. This rigorous selection is made in no cavalier spirit; it is based simply upon recognition of the fact that a poet may profitably repeat himself when a critic may not. We have already examined most of the poetic types that are represented in these two books, and no duplicate specimens are required for our purpose. "The Mill" has been quoted in its entirety; "Avon's Harvest" need not detain us after "Roman Bartholow," whose merits and defects it shares; John Brown, Tasker Norcross, and the Paul of "The Three Taverns" are all figures whose biographies might slip without a jar into any one of Mr. Robinson's earlier collections. "Mr. Flood's Party" would fall into place quite as easily, though it would stand above many of its companions by virtue of its perfect form and kindly humor. But there is one poem that cannot be passed by with casual praise, one that adds measurably to the extent and stature of its author's work. It is "Rembrandt to Rembrandt."

Here is not simply another biographical study of success or failure, in which the old truths are reiterated, and the old judgment is withheld. Here is a fresh and vital statement of the artist's place in nature, by a great poet who is using a great painter as prolocutor. It is Rembrandt who is speaking, in Amsterdam, year 1645, but the voice of Robinson sounds more clearly through the painter's words than is the poet's custom.

Each true artist is possessed of a demon who directs and goads him on; he takes the only way he can, and seldom is it the world's way. He does what he must do in the one way he can do it; neglect, contumely, or approbation may be his reward, but they cannot affect his painting or his writing or his song. With Rembrandt he will contemplate himself and say,

> You made your picture as your demon willed it;
> That's about all of that. Now make as many
> As may be to be made,—for so you will,
> Whatever the toll may be, and hold your light
> So that you see, without so much to blind you
> As even the cobweb-flash of a misgiving,
> Assured and certain that if you see right
> Others will have to see—albeit their seeing
> Shall irk them out of their serenity
> For such a time as umbrage may require.

It is Rembrandt van Ryn who is speaking, and the year is 1645. Saskia van Ulynborch, the lovely Frisian girl who brought him a dowery of forty thousand guilders, bore him four children, and bestowed on him the supreme gift of happiness, has been in her grave for three long years. The painter's new manner, in which the shadow is the thing, is not too popular with his Dutch patrons. But the man must paint, though only God and his own demon can say why. So he stands speaking to a portrait of himself, one of the fifty or the sixty that he put on canvas in his idle hours. No more will Saskia sit upon his knee, as we may see her now, made happy for eternity, within the Dresden Gallery. The world is black, and Hollanders are stupid; but he must paint, and there he stands in oils again. At least his head is still upon his shoulders.

Praise be to God
That you have that; for you are like enough
To need it now, my friend, and from now on;
For there are shadows and obscurities
Immediate or impending on your view,
That may be worse than you have ever painted
For the bewildered and unhappy scorn
Of injured Hollanders in Amsterdam
Who cannot find their fifty florins' worth
Of Holland-face where you have hidden it
In your new golden shadow that excites them,
Or see that when the Lord made color and light
He made not one thing only, or believe
That shadows are not nothing. Saskia said,
Before she died, how they would swear at you,
And in commiseration at themselves.
She laughed a little, too, to think of them—
And then at me. . . . That was before she died.

But she is dead, and now there is only Rembrandt
who remembers her, "and one child beginning to forget"; and with her, so the Dutchmen say, the painter
died.

And here's a fellow painting in the dark,—
A loon who cannot see that he is dead
Before God lets him die. He paints away
At the impossible, so Holland has it,
For venom or for spite, or for defection,
Or else for God knows what. Well, if God knows,
And Rembrandt knows, it matters not so much
What Holland knows or cares. If Holland wants
Its heads all in a row, and all alike,
There's Franz to do them and to do them well—
Rat-catchers, archers, or apothecaries,
And one as like a rabbit as another.

Value received and every Dutchman happy.
All's one to Franz, and to the rest of them,—
Their ways being theirs, are theirs.

He must paint on, and in one way, because a demon
wills it. But what does it all mean? Himself, and all
his pictures?

                     If this be all you are—
This unaccountable aspiring insect—
You'll sleep as easy in oblivion
As any sacred monk or parricide;
And if, as you conceive, you are eternal,
Your soul may laugh, remembering (if a soul
Remembers) your befrenzied aspiration
To smear with certain ochres and some oil
A few more perishable ells of cloth,
And once or twice to square your vanity,
Prove it was you alone that should achieve
A mortal eye—that may, no less, to-morrow
Show an immortal reason why to-day
Men see no more. And what's a mortal eye
More than a mortal herring, who has eyes
As well as you? Why not paint herrings, Rembrandt?

That's the imp who speaks, the incubus perching on
the finished canvas; but then a wiser spirit comes, and
answers in those steady tones: "You made your picture as your demon willed it. . . ." That is the artist's
answer, nor can he ask a better one. As Rembrandt
says to his own likeness, if you sigh

For distant welcome that may not be seen,
Or wayside shouting that will not be heard,
You may as well accommodate your greatness

To the convenience of an easy ditch,
And, anchored there with all your widowed gold,
Forget your darkness in the dark, and hear
No longer the cold wash of Holland scorn.

Here, I should say, is a fit ending to our tale. The evidence is in, and the last words are far from weakest. Of summary or recapitulation there is little need; and each reader is entitled to his own conclusions. Mine are obvious.

It seems to me that there are, even among Robinson's contemporaries, American men and women who have soared as high on lyric wings as he has soared, poets who have dipped for brief moments into a well of human understanding as deep as his, poets who have written lines as beautiful as any he has written; but who among them has produced so large a body of poetry that is so excellent as his? And which of his predecessors, who can match bulk against bulk, can match sustained quality against sustained quality? If, from the work of any other American poet, poems can be selected that will stand head to head with "Captain Craig," "Ben Jonson Entertains a Man from Stratford," "The Man Against the Sky," "Merlin," "Lancelot" and "Rembrandt to Rembrandt," it will be impossible, I believe, to find poems by the same writer that will take equal rank with the great number of really considerable creations that lie between Mr. Robinson's masterpieces. Judge him by the twin measure of fecundity and excellence, and you will know his worth.

The elements that go into the making of a great poet have been defined and catalogued with some precision, but it is still easier to recognize than to explain the synthesis. Try as we will, the nature of the miracle eludes us. In Robinson's case certain facts are obvious, and these, at least, may be noted. His poetry is the product of a thoughtful, enveloping, deeply penetrating mind, that must at times achieve expression in unfamiliar terms and patterns, because it has traveled much alone. He is above all a biographer of souls, who is bound to humanity by the dual bond of sympathy and humor. He is a poet in his rhythmic interpretation of existence, in his conception of the relations of human beings with other human beings and with the universe, and in his ability to marshal thought in language that sustains comparison with the best that has been called poetic. Less egocentric and less subjective than any other poet of his generation, he has, more truly than any other, given us a whole world of his own making. Professor Santayana has lamented that "our poets are things of shreds and patches. They give us episodes and studies, a sketch of this curiosity, a glimpse of that romance. They have no total vision, no grasp of the whole reality, and consequently no capacity for a sane and steady idealization." It is because I believe that Edwin Arlington Robinson has, precisely, this total vision, this grasp, and this consequent capacity, that I can think of him only as the greatest poet whom this country has yet produced. Truly, it was of his kind that Flaubert was thinking, when he wrote to Louise Colet: "Car il y a deux classes de poètes. Les plus grandes, les rares, les vrais maîtres résument l'humanité; sans se preoccuper ni d'eux memes, ni de leurs propres passions,

mettant au rebut leur personalité pour s'absorber dans
celles des autres, ils reproduisent l'Univers, qui se re-
flète dans leurs œuvres, étincelant, varié, multiple,
comme un ciel entier qui se mire dans la mer avec toutes
ses etoiles et tout son azur."

Books by E. A. Robinson

1897—The Children of the Night.
1896—The Torrent and the Night Before.
1902—Captain Craig.
1903—Captain Craig (2nd edition).
1905—The Children of the Night (2nd edition).
1910—The Town Down the River.
1914—Van Zorn.
1915—The Porcupine.
1915—Captain Craig (Revised edition).
1916—The Man Against the Sky.
1917—Merlin.
1919—The Children of the Night (3rd edition).
1920—The Three Taverns.
1920—The Town Down the River (2nd edition).
1920—Lancelot.
1921—Avon's Harvest.
1921—Collected Poems.
1922—Collected Poems (English edition)
1923—Roman Bartholow.
1924—The Man Who Died Twice.
1925—Dionysus In Doubt.

2-171-0